Orion's Star Quilt

Eleanor Burns

For Orion - Our guiding Star!

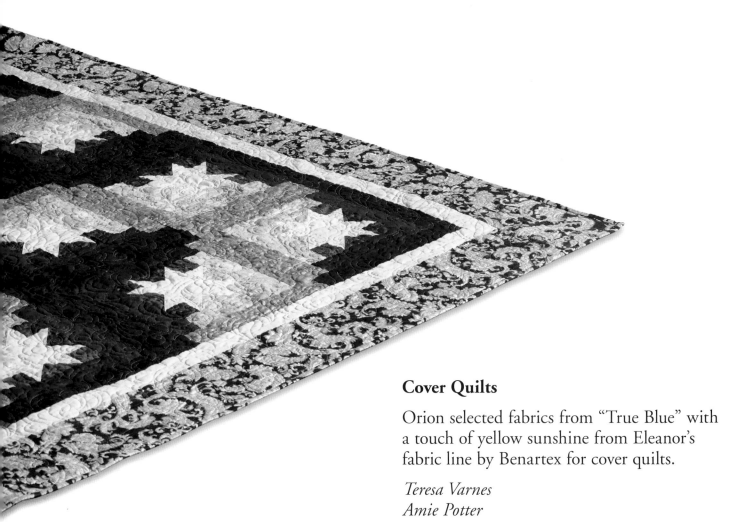

Cover Quilts

Orion selected fabrics from "True Blue" with a touch of yellow sunshine from Eleanor's fabric line by Benartex for cover quilts.

Teresa Varnes
Amie Potter

Pattern Design by Ingrid Wirebjer

First Edition
July, 2009
Published by Quilt in a Day®, Inc.
1955 Diamond Street, San Marcos, CA 92078
©2009 by Eleanor A. Burns Family Trust

ISBN 1-891776-36-3

Art Director: Merritt Voigtlander
Production Artist: Marie Harper

Contents

Introduction

Orion is helping tie our entry of the World's Largest Quilt for Guinness World Records in 1980. By the way, we didn't make it!

As the delivery date for our second child neared, my husband Bill and I pondered over just what to call this new baby boy. We named our first son Grant, a strong masculine name meaning "Great." His brother needed to have as powerful a name.

The answer came when my mother-in-law, Helen Burns, threw a baby shower for me. We played a game with the neighbors, where we had to come up with a name for each letter of the alphabet. Nothing sounded interesting until we got to O – Orion! Orion Burns! Orion the Hunter! Orion the Star! And so Orion the Star joined Grant the Great on November 29, 1975.

I imagined him as a little brave hunter, but instead, he came into the world crying, and kept on crying! For the next year, Orion was in my arms, or in a back pack. I learned to simplify – simplify cooking, cleaning, and even quilting. I had a very short time while Orion napped to get my preparation done for my classes. That's when I developed the term "petal to the metal!" Orion says there would never have been Quilt in a Day had he not been a "crybaby."

It takes just a bit of time to get a great person started, as it happened with Orion the Star, the Incomparable, the Topmost!

Not long after Orion's third birthday, I was faced with raising my sons alone. To make ends meet, we discovered "dumpster digging" for all my stash needs. Since Orion was the littlest, he was the one that was hoisted into the dumpster, and got to toss out the best fabric scraps while Grant and I collected them. I remember the day he stood in the garage looking at boxes of waist band strips we had rescued and said, "Mommy, we are the richest people on the block." Those waist bands went a long way in making strip quilts. Our favorite was a Rail Fence with bright reds, yellows, and blues created while both Grant and Orion were home with chicken pox. Years later, Orion pulled a quilt out of a dumpster while boating at Lake Havasu, and claimed it was the prettiest quilt he had ever seen.

With Grant already in elementary school, Orion and I headed off to teach quilting to survive. Only knee high to a cash register, he assisted me selling Quilt in a Day books at quilt fairs and classes, lugged boxes, and carried quilts.

Growing up in the industry, it's not surprising that Orion is now the General Manager of Quilt in a Day, always there with a galaxy of fresh ideas - a leader, a creator, a star! Through his numerous e-mails, Orion met Ingrid Wirebjer and became interested in her quilt design. Combining the Burns "signature" block, the log cabin, with a Star, it was natural to name the block after him. Not only is Orion heading my company, but he founded and leads the San Diego Shop Hop with 17 shops.

Orion is still a kid at heart, always adventurous and willing to contribute. A Chicken dancing the Chicken Dance, a soldier swinging to Boogie Woogie Bugle Boy, Bob Hope entertaining with jokes, Pretty Woman strutting her stuff, or ice cream soda jerk,… he has done them all, and doesn't seem to get embarrassed. He's a good sport, endlessly posing for photos.

This star is for you, Orion Burns! the Hunter! the Superstar!

Orion's ice cream parlor won "Most Creative Booth Award" at 2000 Quilt Market.

Eleanor Burns

About the Quilt

Orion's Star Quilt combines two traditional, well loved blocks into an exciting new look. The center part of the block is an eight pointed Star, often referred to as the Evening Star, or Sawtooth Star. Its less common name is Simple Star, and with the easy "flying geese" method used to make star points, the star is certainly simple to make.

The Log Cabin completes Orion's Star block. Strips are assembly-line sewn around the star in a "log cabin" technique using different values of two colors. The finished size of the Star is 8" square. Once "logs" are added, the finished size of the block is 16" square.

The single triangles on the inside of Star Points and Star Corners are sewn in the lightest values, creating a diagonal line through the block. The Log Cabin strips continue this division of color throughout the block.

Once blocks are assembled, they can be turned and set together in a variety of different patterns. Blocks in this Lap quilt are set together in the traditional Fields and Furrows pattern.

In this example, the green Evening Star is surrounded with different values of yellow and blue Log Cabin strips.

Fields and Furrows
Teresa Varnes
Amie Potter
61" x 77"

Fabric Selection

Selecting fabric for Orion's Star Quilt is the same as selecting fabrics for a traditional Log Cabin Quilt. The Star represents the Log Cabin hearth. The three values in one color on one side are the sun in front of the cabin. The three values in a second color on the opposite side are the shadow behind the cabin.

For inspiration, begin by selecting a multi-colored fabric. From that one fabric, pick the Star color and two dominant complimentary colors for the "logs." For clarity in design, select fabrics contrasting with each other.

Choose a print for the Star that appears solid from a distance, or tone on tone. When choosing additional fabric, select three different values with gradual change for each color. **Avoid big jumps in value change.** In addition, mix scales of prints, as a small scale print, a large-scale print, and a texture or print that looks solid from a distance. A quilt of all the same scale fabrics tends to look "boring."

A large-scale print used in the blocks, or an additional large-scale print, is striking when used in Borders.

It's best to purchase yardage as opposed to fat quarters. There's too much waste in a fat quarter because of the length of the 20" half strip. If you must use a fat quarter, piece half strips together first into one longer strip.

In this example, the Star is a rich dark brown, surrounded in three earth values on the light side, and three sky values on the dark side.

The second dark fabric pulls in earth tones from the opposite side.

The Border print provided inspiration for fabric selection.

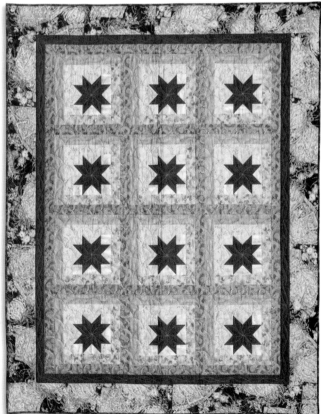

*All Sevens
Sue Bouchard
Amie Potter
61" x 77"*

Gallery of Quilts

Each quilter put her own creative touch to these quilts.

Grandma's Choice

Perfect for a baby boy, Teresa's crib size quilt is cute with a well-proportioned mix of colors. Shining yellow stars are framed in small scale green check on one side of the block, and deeper blue plaid on the opposite side. All geometric prints for grandma's special guy!

Teresa Varnes
Amie Potter
45" x 61"

Super Nova

LuAnn selected the attractive large scale, multi-colored fabric first, and used it for the Second Dark in the blocks and Second Border. The colors of the four pastel Stars were also pulled from that one print. Since two stars alike are made at a time, LuAnn ended up with two identical quilts! See page 32 for explanation of how two stars are made at the same time. The sunny yellow First Border, quilted with feathers, pulled all fabrics together beautifully.

LuAnn Stout
Robin Kinley
45" x 45"

8

Birds in My Garden

The Birdhouse theme fabric featured a variety of blocks for the 4½" "fussy cut" Star Center plus a Border print. Using colors in the novelty print, lights and darks were chosen to pull the quilt top together. Dark burgundy Star Points create a contrast with log fabrics.

When using a directional "fussy cut" Star Center, decide how you want your blocks laid out. The All Sevens pattern works well, because you layout your blocks in one direction.

The directional Border print is most effective if you place all your flowers growing from the center out and miter the corners.

Fussy Cut 4½" Center

Sue Bouchard
Amie Potter
60" x 60"

Pretty Ballerinas

Any little girl would love these colorful ballerinas dancing across the Stars and Border! Anne "fussy cut" graceful dancers into 4½" Centers for Stars. Bright pink Star Points keep focus on the performers, and a softer pink and green were repeated for "logs." A charming stripe surrounds the recital!

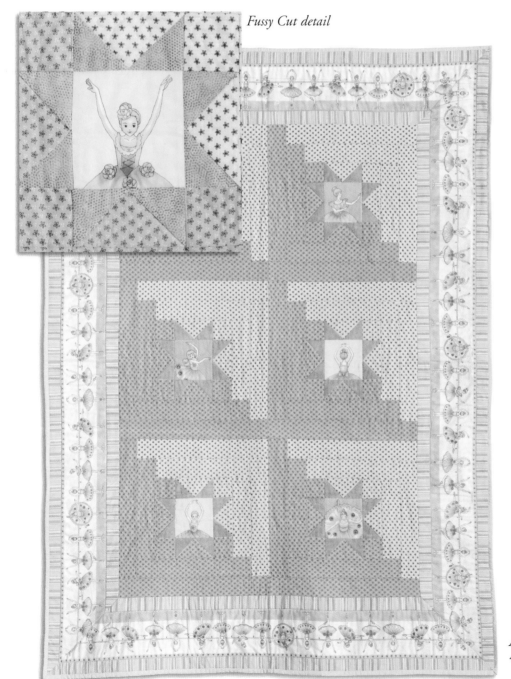

Fussy Cut detail

Border detail

Anne Dease
45" x 61"

"One Year Later"

Black, white and fuchsia pink were the colors chosen for Sue's son, Dylan and her daughter-in-law, Kelli's wedding in 2008. They were not Sue's favorite combination, but after working with the color grouping while preparing for the big event, she found them fun and dramatic to work with.

Sue chose three black on white fabrics, and three white on black fabrics and combined them with bright pink Stars to make a modern interpretation of the Orion's Star Quilt. She made extra Star Points and turned them into a unique border treatment to compliment the Stars.

Sue Bouchard
Amie Potter
46" x 65"

Dancing Daisies

Heavily contrasting vibrant yellow and verdant green "logs" compliment the border of daisies printed on black background. Linda artistically sewed perky black Star Points around festive daisy Center Squares. To break up dark lines in the "logs," Linda used darker values before medium values in the blocks. Robin quilted graceful feathers meandering among "Fields and Furrows!"

Linda Parker
Robin Kinley
61" x 77"

Ann Drothler
Amie Potter
61" x 77"

Caterpillars

Bright orange batik Stars set this Lap on fire, with softer yellow "logs" aglow on half of the blocks. The forest green brings even more life into this quilt skillfully pieced by Ann Drothler. Amie free motioned Stars in the Center and stitched in the ditch ¼" away with variegated thread. Fanciful feathers circle the Stars!

13

Yardage and Cutting Charts

The term "strip" refers to a strip of fabric cut selvage to selvage, which is between 40" to 45" in length. Yardage amounts and number of strips are based on a 40" selvage to selvage strip. If your strips are longer than 40", you may have enough fabric left on a strip to complete an extra block.

Wallhanging
45" x 45"
Four Blocks
2 x 2

Sunny Days

In sunny day yellow and rich blue night, this Wallhanging is perfect for a patio room wall. It's simply quilted with stitch in the ditch around the Stars and ¼" from seams in the logs. Free motion flowers float across the lovely Border. Any novice can achieve success!

All Sevens
Teresa Varnes
Amie Potter

Stars	⅜ yd
Star Points	(1) 7" strip cut into (4) 7" squares
Star Centers	(1) 4½" strip cut into (4) 4½" squares
First Light	¼ yd
Star Points	(1) 5½" strip cut into (2) 5½" squares
Star Corners	(4) 2½" squares
Second Light	⅓ yd
Blocks	(3) 2½" strips
Third Light	⅓ yd
Blocks	(3) 2½" strips

First Dark	⅓ yd
Star Points	(1) 5½" strip cut into (2) 5½" squares
Star Corners	(1) 2½" strip cut into (12) 2½" squares
Second Dark	⅓ yd
Blocks	(3) 2½" strips
Third Dark	⅜ yd
Blocks	(4) 2½" strips
First Border	⅓ yd
	(4) 2" strips
Second Border	⅝ yd
	(4) 4" strips
Binding	½ yd
	(5) 3" strips
Backing	3 yds
Batting	53" x 53"

Crib
45" x 61"
Six Blocks
2 x 3

Waiting for Jonas

Jimna combined juvenile fabrics for her precious expected son Jonas with cool colors of the ocean. Amie paid tribute to the Burns' coastal home with suns quilted in the centers of the Stars, swells of the ocean in the "logs," and waves on the First Border. As a special treat, Jonas will enjoy the sailboats floating across the Second Border!

Jonas Jacob Burns — due September 1, 2009.

Fields and Furrows
Jimna Burns
Amie Potter

Stars	5/8 yd
Star Points	(2) 7" strips cut into (6) 7" squares
Star Centers	(1) 4½" strip cut into (6) 4½" squares
First Light	1/3 yd
Star Points	(1) 5½" strip cut into (3) 5½" squares
Star Corners	(1) 2½" strip cut into (6) 2½" squares
Second Light	3/8 yd
Blocks	(4) 2½" strips
Third Light	½ yd
Blocks	(5) 2½" strips

First Dark	3/8 yd
Star Points	(1) 5½" strip cut into (3) 5½" squares
Star Corners	(2) 2½" strips cut into (18) 2½" squares
Second Dark	3/8 yd
Blocks	(4) 2½" strips
Third Dark	½ yd
Blocks	(6) 2½" strips
First Border	½ yd
	(5) 2½" strips
Second Border	1 yd
	(6) 5" strips
Binding	¾ yd
	(6) 3" strips
Backing	3 yds
Batting	53" x 69"

15

Lap
61" x 77"
Twelve Blocks
3 x 4

Autumn Harvest

Judy's striking quilt sings out in seven tones of rich harvest colors. Deep pumpkin Stars contrast with soft wheat and vibrant squash colors. Cousin Carol quilted gorgeous feathers through the wheat field, and stitched in the ditch through the squash patch of paisley and plaid. Abundant with beauty!

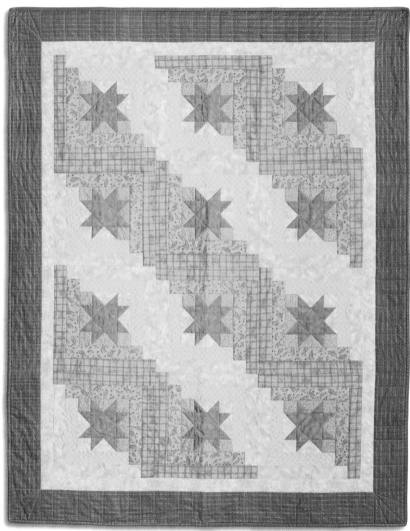

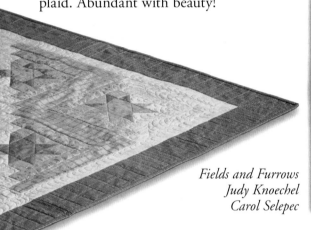

Fields and Furrows
Judy Knoechel
Carol Selepec

Stars	1 yd
Star Points	(3) 7" strips cut into (12) 7" squares
Star Centers	(2) 4½" strips cut into (12) 4½" squares
First Light	**⅓ yd**
Star Points	(1) 5½" strip cut into (6) 5½" squares
Star Corners	(1) 2½" strip cut into (12) 2½" squares
Second Light	**⅝ yd**
Blocks	(7) 2½" strips
Third Light	**⅞ yd**
Blocks	(10) 2½" strips

First Dark	½ yd
Star Points	(1) 5½" strip cut into (6) 5½" squares
Star Corners	(3) 2½" strips cut into (36) 2½" squares
Second Dark	**⅔ yd**
Blocks	(8) 2½" strips
Third Dark	**1 yd**
Blocks	(12) 2½" strips
First Border	**½ yd**
	(6) 2½" strips
Second Border	**1⅛ yds**
	(7) 5" strips
Binding	**¾ yd**
	(7) 3" strips
Backing	**4¾ yds**
Batting	**69" x 85"**

Twin

72" x 104"
Fifteen Blocks
3 x 5

To Dream On

Intense red Stars are abundant floating across a winter beige and black sky. Martha selected similar values with varying scales to carry out the striking design. Amie quilted turning leaves and a trailing vine through the Borders. Striking!

Fields and Furrows
Martha Hernandez
Amie Potter

Stars	1⅛ yds
Star Points	(4) 7" strips cut into (16) 7" squares
Star Centers	(2) 4½" strips cut into (15) 4½" squares
First Light	**½ yd**
Star Points	(2) 5½" strips cut into (8) 5½" squares
Star Corners	(1) 2½" strip cut into (15) 2½" squares
Second Light	**¾ yd**
Blocks	(9) 2½" strips
Third Light	**1 yd**
Blocks	(13) 2½" strips

First Dark	⅝ yd
Star Points	(2) 5½" strips cut into (8) 5½" squares
Star Corners	(3) 2½" strips cut into (45) 2½" squares
Second Dark	**⅞ yd**
Blocks	(10) 2½" strips
Third Dark	**1¼ yds**
Blocks	(16) 2½" strips
First Border	⅝ yd (7) 2½" strips
Second Border	1 yd (8) 4" strips
Third Border	1⅞ yds (9) 7" strips
Binding	1 yd (9) 3" strips
Backing	6¼ yds
Batting	80" x 112"

17

Square Queen with Pillow Shams
98" x 98"
Sixteen Blocks
4 x 4

I Can't Wait Till Christmas

Angela fell in love with this Christmas line from Benartex called "I believe in Santa." Cheery red Stars with light holly leaves and green Christmas Tree balls sing out holiday cheer! Festive! Carol quilted feathers in the light triangular shapes, and cross hatched large green areas. Dancing Stars and holly fill out the pattern!

Negative/Positive
Angela Castro
Carol Selepec

Pillow Sham instructions are on page 87.

Stars	1¼ yds
Star Points	(4) 7" strips cut into (16) 7" squares
Star Centers	(2) 4½" strips cut into (16) 4½" squares
First Light	⅝ yd
Star Points	(2) 5½" strips cut into (8) 5½" squares
Star Corners	(2) 2½" strips cut into (16) 2½" squares
Second Light	⅞ yd
Blocks	(10) 2½" strips
Third Light	1¼ yds
Blocks	(14) 2½" strips

Pillow Shams*	2⅞ yds
Top	(2) 28" x 34"
Backing	(4) 21" x 28"
Batting	1¾ yds
	(2) 28" x 34"

* *Makes two*

First Dark	⅝ yd
Star Points	(2) 5½" strips cut into (8) 5½" squares
Star Corners	(3) 2½" strips cut into (48) 2½" squares
Second Dark	1 yd
Blocks	(12) 2½" strips
Third Dark	1⅓ yds
Blocks	(16) 2½" strips
First Border	⅞ yd
	(8) 3½" strips
Second Border	1½ yds
	(8) 6" strips
Third Border	2½ yds
	(9) 9" strips
Binding	1 yd
	(10) 3" strips
Backing	9 yds
Batting	106" x 106"

Rectangular Queen
98" x 114"
Twenty Blocks
4 x 5

Blooming Stars

Karen loves yellow! Her first choice in fabric was the large scale, multi-colored print on green background. Vivid colors of yellow, green, and pink were pulled from the detailed floral print. A coordinating small-scale print was used for Third Light. The Zig Zag pattern fits perfectly on the top of her queen size bed!

Zig Zag
Karen Pavone
Amie Potter

Stars	1⅓ yds
Star Points	(4) 7" strips cut into (20) 7" squares
Star Centers	(3) 4½" strips cut into (20) 4½" squares
First Light	⅝ yd
Star Points	(2) 5½" strips cut into (10) 5½" squares
Star Corners	(2) 2½" strips cut into (20) 2½" squares
Second Light	1 yd
Blocks	(12) 2½" strips
Third Light	1⅓ yds
Blocks	(17) 2½" strips

First Dark	¾ yd
Star Points	(2) 5½" strips cut into (10) 5½" squares
Star Corners	(4) 2½" strips cut into (60) 2½" squares
Second Dark	1⅛ yd
Blocks	(14) 2½" strips
Third Dark	1½ yds
Blocks	(20) 2½" strips
First Border	⅞ yd (8) 3½" strips
Second Border	1⅝ yds (9) 6" strips
Third Border	2¾ yds (10) 9" strips
Binding	1 yd (10) 3" strips
Backing	9 yds
Batting	106" x 122"

19

California King
112" x 112"
Twenty-Five Blocks
5 x 5

Oriental Galaxy

Subtle blue and peach mums and cherry blossoms outlined in gold set the theme for Teresa's stunning oriental quilt. The large and small-scale flowers printed on lacy backgrounds appear to be gently floating. Teresa found it easiest to repeat the same light peach than select additional fabrics. For more interest, she made Stars in two different colors. Simply divide the number of Stars needed by two, and purchase one 7" square and one 4½" square for each.

Fields and Furrows
Teresa Varnes
Amie Potter

Stars	1⅔ yds
Star Points	(6) 7" strips cut into (26) 7" squares
Star Centers	(3) 4½" strips cut into (25) 4½" squares
First Light	**⅝ yd**
Star Points	(2) 5½" strips cut into (13) 5½" squares
Star Corners	(2) 2½" strips cut into (25) 2½" squares
Second Light	**1¼ yds**
Blocks	(16) 2½" strips
Third Light	**1⅝ yds**
Blocks	(22) 2½" strips

First Dark	¾ yd
Star Points	(2) 5½" strips cut into (13) 5½" squares
Star Corners	(5) 2½" strips cut into (75) 2½" squares
Second Dark	**1⅓ yds**
Blocks	(18) 2½" strips
Third Dark	**2 yds**
Blocks	(26) 2½" strips
First Border	1 yd (9) 3½" strips
Second Border	1⅝ yds (10) 5" strips
Third Border	3 yds (11) 9" strips
Binding	1⅛ yds (11) 3" strips
Backing	9½ yds
Batting	119" x 119"

Dual King
121" x 121"
Thirty-Six Blocks
6 x 6

Orion's Starry Night

Karyn aimed high for a glittery Star in the dark night Sky. Envisioning a swirling galaxy, Karyn selected the Whirligig layout. The First Light shimmers in a light blue metallic, while Darks contrast in deep tone on tone.

Karyn add only two borders to fit her bed.

Whirligig
Karyn Helsel
Phyllis Strickland

Stars	2¼ yds
Star Points	(8) 7" strips cut into (36) 7" squares
Star Centers	(5) 4½" strips cut into (36) 4½" squares
First Light	**¾ yd**
Star Points	(3) 5½" strips cut into (18) 5½" squares
Star Corners	(3) 2½" strips cut into (36) 2½" squares
Second Light	**1⅝ yds**
Blocks	(21) 2½" strips
Third Light	**2¼ yds**
Blocks	(30) 2½" strips

First Dark	1⅛ yds
Star Points	(3) 5½" strips cut into (18) 5½" squares
Star Corners	(7) 2½" strips cut into (108) 2½" squares
Second Dark	**1¾ yds**
Blocks	(24) 2½" strips
Third Dark	**2⅔" yds**
Blocks	(36) 2½" strips
First Border	¾ yd (10) 2½" strips
Second Border	1½ yds (11) 4½" strips
Third Border	2½ yds (12) 7" strips
Binding	1¼ yds (13) 3" strips
Backing	10½ yds
Batting	129" x 129"

Paste-Up Sheet

You have permission to photocopy this page. Cut each fabric to size, and glue in place. Keep this sheet beside your sewing machine while sewing blocks.

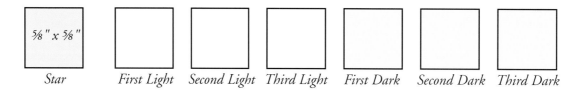

⅝" x ⅝"						
Star	First Light	Second Light	Third Light	First Dark	Second Dark	Third Dark

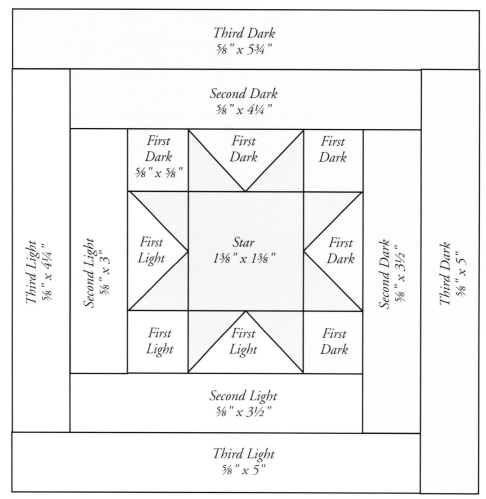

Audition your fabrics before cutting out your quilt. After pasting fabric strips in place, make at least four color photocopies of the pasted-up block. Trim out blocks, and place in different layouts. View from a distance to check fabric and color choices.

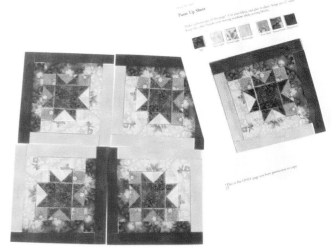

22

Supplies

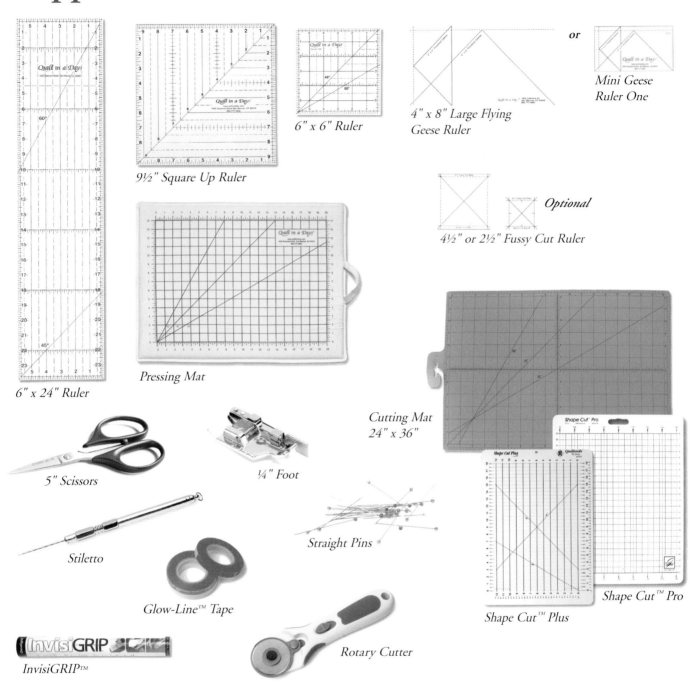

9½" Square Up Ruler

6" x 6" Ruler

4" x 8" Large Flying Geese Ruler

or

Mini Geese Ruler One

Optional

4½" or 2½" Fussy Cut Ruler

Pressing Mat

6" x 24" Ruler

Cutting Mat 24" x 36"

Shape Cut™ Pro

Shape Cut™ Plus

5" Scissors

¼" Foot

Stiletto

Straight Pins

Glow-Line™ Tape

InvisiGRIP™

Rotary Cutter

Supplies for Machine Quilting on Conventional Sewing Machine

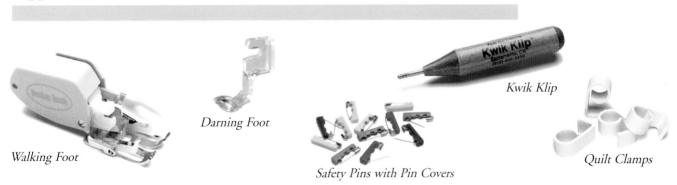

Walking Foot

Darning Foot

Safety Pins with Pin Covers

Kwik Klip

Quilt Clamps

23

Cutting

Cutting 7" Strips for Star Points

The best ruler to use for cutting strips selvage to selvage is the 6" x 24" Ruler. For cutting 7" wide strips, use inch marks on cutting mat along with ruler.

1. Place gridded cutting mat with mat's zero mark in bottom left corner.

2. Place fabric on mat with folded edge along top horizontal line, and left edge slightly to left of zero.

3. To straighten edge, place 6" x 24" ruler along edge of fabric at zero markings.

4. Spread your fingers and place four on top of ruler with little finger on mat to keep ruler firmly in place.

5. Starting below fabric, cut away from you, applying pressure on ruler and cutter. Keep blade next to ruler's edge.

6. Pick up and move ruler to right. Line up edge of ruler with 7" marks on mat.

7. Cut designated number of 7" strips following Yardage and Cutting Charts.

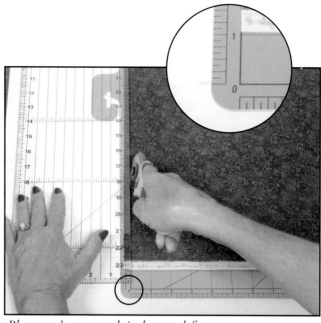

Place mat's zero mark in bottom left corner. Straighten left edge.

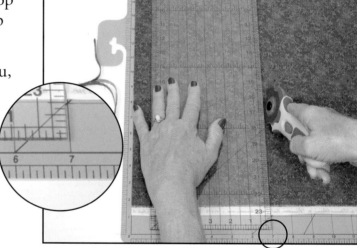

Move ruler and cut strips 7" wide.

Cutting 7" Strips into 7" Squares

1. Turn strip and square off left edge.

2. Place 9½" Square Up Ruler on strip with 1" in upper right corner. Line up 7" mark with left edge of strip.

3. Cut into 7" squares with 9½" Square Up Ruler.

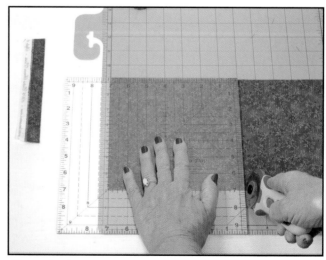

Cut strips into squares.

Cutting 4½" Strips with 6" x 24" Ruler

Use measurements on 6" x 24" Ruler to cut strips less than 6" wide.

1. Turn 6" x 24" Ruler to bottom side. Cut loff piece of Glow-Line™ Tape same length as ruler.

2. Place tape on bottom side of ruler at 4½" line.

3. Cut piece of Invisigrip ½" smaller than ruler. Place on bottom side of ruler. Invisigrip keeps the ruler from sliding when cutting.

4. Place fabric on mat with folded edge along a top horizontal line, and left edge on a vertical line.

5. Straighten left edge. Move ruler and line up with 4½" line.

6. Cut designated number of 4½" strips following Yardage and Cutting Charts.

7. Continue to cut designated number and width of strips.

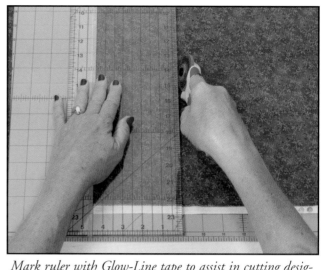

Mark ruler with Glow-Line tape to assist in cutting designated widths of strips.

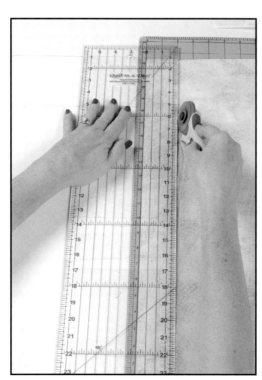

If you are right-handed, the fabric should trail off to the right.

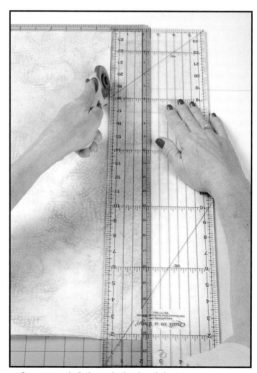

If you are left-handed, the fabric should trail off to the left.

Cutting Strips with Shape Cut™

Select between two different Shape Cut rulers:

- **Shape Cut Plus Ruler**
- **Shape Cut Pro Ruler**

*The Shape Cut Plus is a 12" x 18" slotted ruler for cutting **folded fabric** into selvage to selvage strips at ½" increments.*

1. Place Glow-Line™ Tape at designated measurement.

2. **Fold fabric into fourths**, lining up fold with selvage edges.

3. Place Shape Cut™ on fabric. Line up zero horizontal line with bottom edge of fabric. Allow extra fabric to left of zero vertical line for straightening.

4. Place blade of cutter in zero slot, and straighten left edge of fabric. Cut strips at designated widths.

5. Cut Borders according to Yardage Charts.

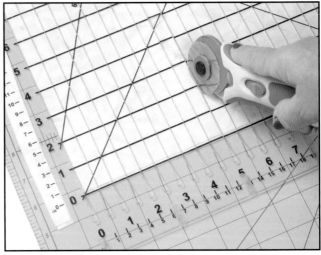

Line up zero horizontal line with bottom edge of fabric. Place rotary blade in designated slot and cut.

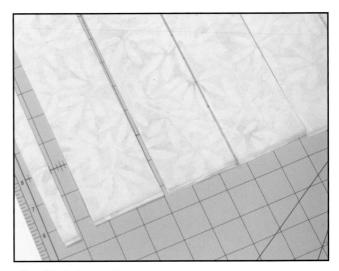

Cut fabric into strips.

Cutting 2½" Strips with Shape Cut Pro™

*The Shape Cut Pro is a large 20" x 23" slotted ruler for cutting **folded 20"** widths of fabric into 2½" selvage to selvage strips.*

1. Stack Second Dark and then Second Light fabric on cutting mat, lining up selvage edges with zero horizontal line on mat.

2. Place Shape Cut™ Pro on fabric. Line up zero horizontal line with bottom edge of fabric. Allow extra fabric to left of vertical zero for straightening.

3. Place blade of cutter in zero slot, and straighten left edge of fabric.

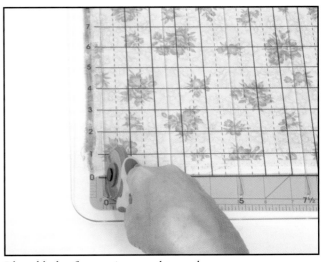

Place blade of cutter in zero slot, and straighten left edge of fabric.

4. Cut strips for blocks at 2½" according to Yardage and Cutting Charts.

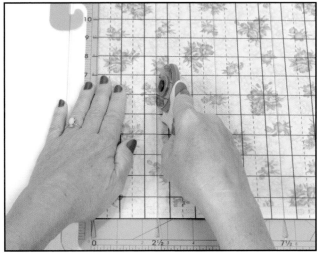

Place cutter in slots, and cut 2½" strips.

5. Cut Second Light until you have enough for your particular size. Continue cutting Second Dark strips

Cut all Second Light strips.

6. Stack.

7. Repeat layering and cutting Third Light and Third Dark 2½" strips for blocks, with Third Dark on bottom.

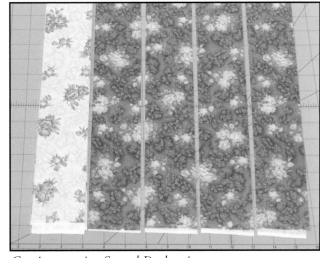

Continue cutting Second Dark strips.

Fussy Cuts for Your Stars

A fussy cut is a selected image, such as a flower, centered on your patch. With a Fussy Cut Ruler™, you can cut the identical image repeatedly with ease.

There are two sizes of Fussy Cut Rulers available for Orion's Star: 2½" and 4½". Perfect places for the Fussy Cuts are the 4½" Star Center or four 2½" Corners of your Star block.

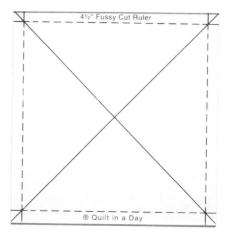

Fussy Cut 2½" Corners

Fussy Cut 4½" Center

How to Make a Fussy Cut

1. To keep ruler from slipping while cutting, cut InvisiGRIP™ ½" smaller than ruler and press on bottom side.

2. Find image on fabric that fits within size needed.

3. Place ruler on top of image, with center of X on center of image. The dashed lines indicate the seam lines. Shift ruler so image fits within seam lines.

4. If it's critical that each image be identical, place a piece of InvisiGRIP on top side of Fussy Cut Ruler. Trace outline of fussy cut on the top piece with a permanent marking pen. Remove top InvisiGRIP after cutting all your squares.

5. Cut around ruler with rotary cutter. To help with accuracy, place fabric on Brooklyn Revolver™ or Olfa Rotating Mat.

6. Move ruler to next fussy cut, line up ruler on image, and repeat.

¼" Seam Allowance Test

Use a consistent ¼" seam allowance throughout the construction of your quilt. If necessary, adjust the needle position, change the presser foot, or feed the fabric under the presser foot to achieve the ¼".

1. Cut three 1½" x 6" pieces.

2. Place a fine, sharp #70/10 Schmetz Universal needle on your machine. Set machine at 15 stitches per inch, or 2.0 on computerized machine.

3. Thread your machine with a good quality of neutral shade polyester or cotton spun thread.

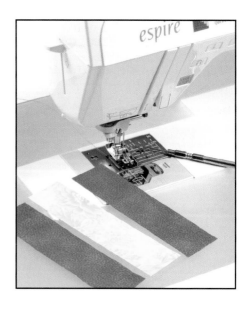

4. Sew three strips together lengthwise with what you think is a ¼" seam.

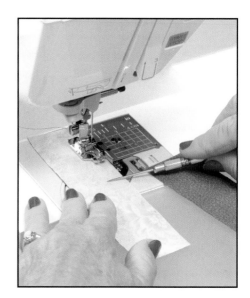

5. Press seams in one direction. Make sure no folds occur at seams.

6. Place sewn sample under a ruler and measure it's width. It should measure exactly 3½". If sample measures smaller than 3½", seam is too large. If sample measures larger than 3½", seam is too small. Adjust seam and repeat if necessary.

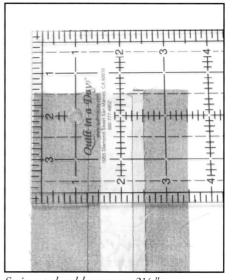

Strip set should measure 3½".

¼" Foot

A ¼" foot is available for most sewing machines from your sewing machine dealer. It has a guide on it to help keep your fabric from straying, thus giving you perfect ¼" seams. Your patchwork is then consistently accurate.

It's important that your seams are consistent!

If you don't have a ¼" foot, these tools are useful.

- Adhesive Strip
- Post-it® Notes

From center of hole to inside edge of guide, width is ¼".

Adhesive Strip

Place adhesive strip against multi-purpose foot. Move needle so it is ¼" from edge of adhesive strip. Sew with fabric against adhesive strip for accurate and consistent seams.

Place adhesive strip against multi-purpose foot.

Post-it® Notes

Stick a partial stack of notes ¼" away from needle. Sew with strips against stack of notes.

Move needle ¼" from edge of stack and sew.

31

Making Stars

The Star block is made of four 2½" x 4½" Star Points, one 4½" Center square, and four 2½" Corner squares. The finished size of the Star block is 8" square.

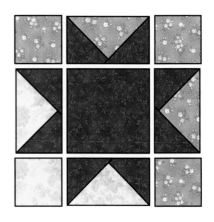

All four Star Points are the same fabric. However, two different fabrics are used for the single triangle inside the Star Points. The first fabric for the single triangle is First Light. The second fabric is First Dark. Only one 2½" Corner square is First Light. The remaining three 2½" Corner squares are First Dark. The use of these two fabrics in Star Points begins the division of the two contrasting "logs."

The technique used for sewing Star Points creates four identical points at a time.

 =  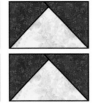  =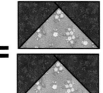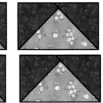

Only two of each are needed for one block. Four Points from each fabric are divided into two Star blocks.

To check the fabric, complete the two Stars before starting on your quilt.

Cutting for Two 8" Stars	
Stars	
Points	(2) 7" squares
Centers	(2) 4½" squares
First Light	
Points	(1) 5½" square
Corners	(2) 2½" squares
First Dark	
Points	(1) 5½" square
Corners	(6) 2½" squares

Making Two Scrappy Blocks

1. For scrappy 16" finished size blocks, cut individual pieces following chart. Logs can be different fabrics, as long as two sides contrast.

Two 16" Scrappy Blocks	
Stars	
Points	(2) 7" squares
Centers	(2) 4½" squares
First Light	
Points	(1) 5½" square
Corners	(2) 2½" squares
First Dark	
Points	(1) 5½" square
Corners	(6) 2½" squares
Second Light	(2) 2½" x 8½"
	(2) 2½" x 10½"
Second Dark	(2) 2½" x 10½"
	(2) 2½" x 12½"
Third Light	(2) 2½" x 12½"
	(2) 2½" x 14½"
Third Dark	(2) 2½" x 14½"
	(2) 2½" x 16½"

See directions for Scrappy Quilt beginning on page 88.

Teresa Varnes
Amie Potter
61" x 77"

2. Sew Stars two at a time following directions beginning on page 34.

3. Lay out "logs" and assembly-line sew following directions beginning on page 50.

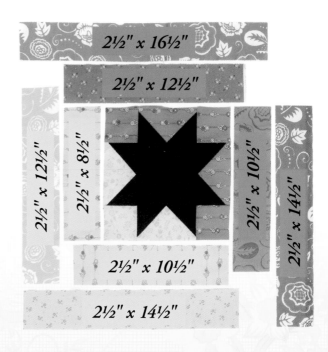

2½" x 16½"
2½" x 12½"
2½" x 12½"
2½" x 8½"
2½" x 10½"
2½" x 14½"
2½" x 10½"
2½" x 14½"

Marking Star Points

1. Divide 7" squares for Star Points into two equal stacks.

Squares in Each Stack	
Wallhanging	2 each
Crib	3 each
Lap	6 each
Twin	8 each
Square Queen	8 each
Rectangular Queen	10 each
California King	13 each
Dual King	18 each

Make two equal stacks.
Example is for a Four Block Wallhanging.

2. Stack 5½" First Light squares with left stack.

3. Repeat with 5½" First Dark squares with right stack.

4. Place one 5½" First Light square **right sides together** and centered on one 7" Star Points square.

5. Repeat with one 5½" First Dark square.

Center 5½" squares on 7" Star Point Squares, right sides together.

Follow these steps to help center 5½" squares on 7" squares.

6.   Place 6" x 12" Ruler on squares with 45° line on bottom edge. The 5½" square is centered if ruler touches through four corners. If necessary, tweak until it is centered.

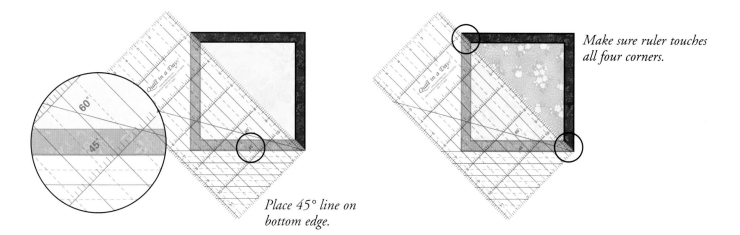

Place 45° line on bottom edge.

Make sure ruler touches all four corners.

7.   **For additional help**, use a cutting mat with a 45° line. Place squares on cutting mat, and line up corners of squares with 45° line.

8.   Draw diagonal line across squares. Pin.

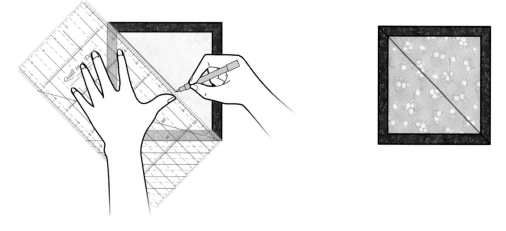

9.   Repeat for remaining squares.

Sewing Star Points

1. Place ¼" foot on sewing machine.

2. Sew ¼" from left side of drawn line. Use 15 stitches per inch or 2.0 on computerized machine.

3. Assembly-line sew all squares.

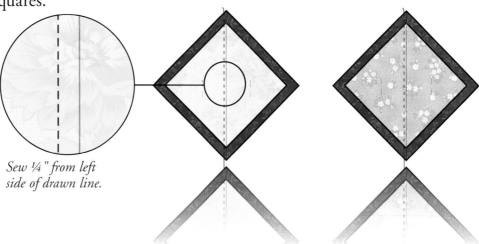

Sew ¼" from left side of drawn line.

4. **Turn squares.** Assembly-line sew ¼" from line on second side. Distance between two lines of stitching is ½".

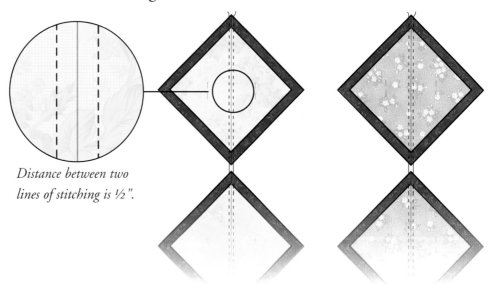

Distance between two lines of stitching is ½".

5. Clip connecting threads. Remove pins.

6. Cut on drawn line and stack. Keep two fabrics separated.

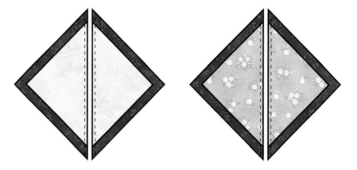

Pressing Triangles

1. Place on pressing mat with **large triangle on top**. Set seam by pressing **stitches**.

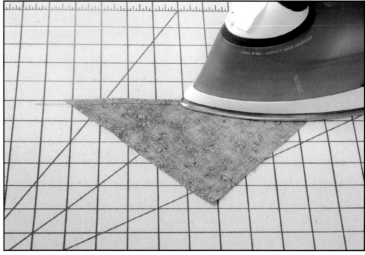

Place large triangle wrong side up. Set seam by pressing stitches.

2. Open and **press toward large triangle**. Check that there are no tucks in seam.

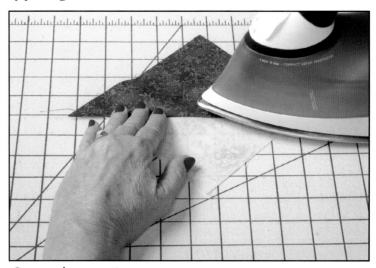

Open and press against seam.

3. Check on back side. Seam is pressed toward **large triangle**.

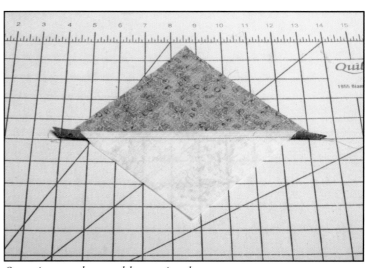

Seam is pressed toward large triangle.

Sewing Star Points

1. Place pieces right sides together so that opposite fabrics touch. Match Star Points with First Light and Star Points with First Dark. **Seams are parallel with each other.**

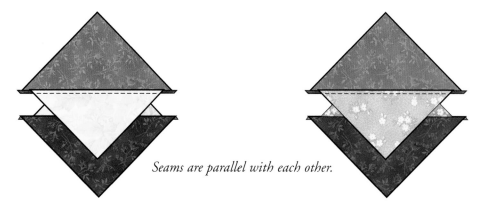

Seams are parallel with each other.

2. Match up outside edges. Notice that there is a gap between seams. **The seams do not lock.**

Seams do not lock.

3. Draw a vertical line across seams. Pin.

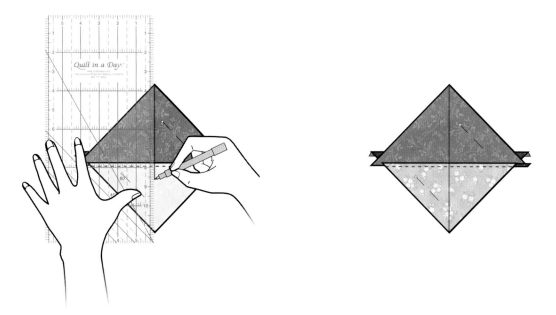

4. Sew ¼" from both sides of drawn line. Hold seams flat with stiletto so seams do not flip.

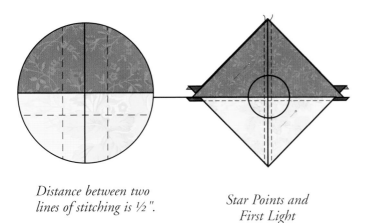

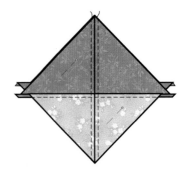

Distance between two lines of stitching is ½".

Star Points and First Light

Star Points and First Dark

5. Remove pins. Press to set seam.

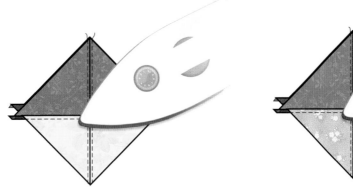

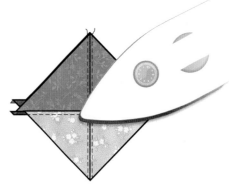

6. Cut on drawn line.

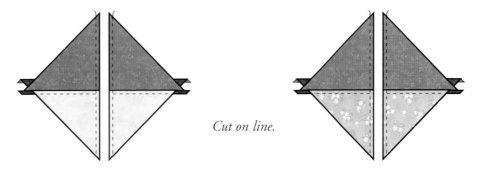

Cut on line.

Pressing Star Points

1. Fold in half. Match tips.

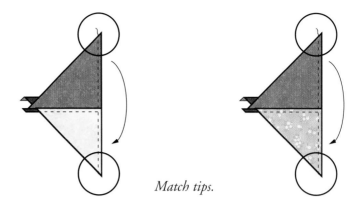

Match tips.

2. Clip to stitching.

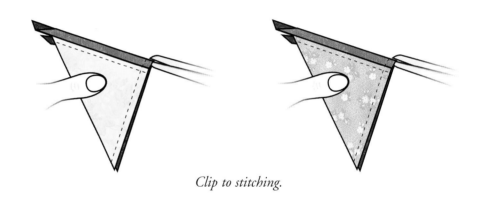

Clip to stitching.

3. Open Star Points. This clip
    allows seam allowance to be
    pressed away from single triangle.

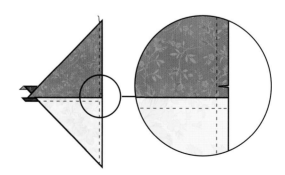

4. From right side, place tip of iron on single triangle of First Light. Press into Star Points.

5. Turn and press into second Star Point on opposite side.

6. Repeat with First Dark, pressing from single triangle into Star Point.

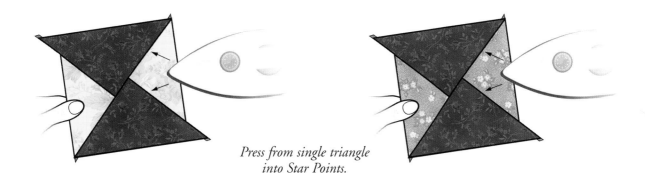

*Press from single triangle
into Star Points.*

7. Turn over, and press on wrong side. At clipped seam, fabric is pressed in opposite directions.

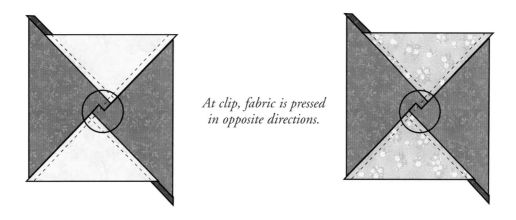

*At clip, fabric is pressed
in opposite directions.*

8. Re-press if seams do not lay flat as illustrated.

Squaring Up Star Points

Star Points are oversized and need to be trimmed to **2" x 4" finished size** using one of the following Geese Rulers from Quilt in a Day. **Size of patch with seam allowance included is 2½" x 4½".**

Mini Geese Ruler One

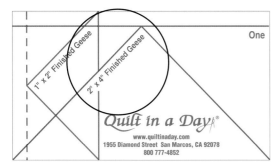

*Mini Geese Ruler One is easiest to use, with least amount of turning. When squaring Star Points to 2" x 4" finished size, use **green lines** on Mini Geese Ruler. This ruler is small and harder to hold onto, but you can trim all the way around the ruler without picking it up.*

Large Flying Geese Ruler

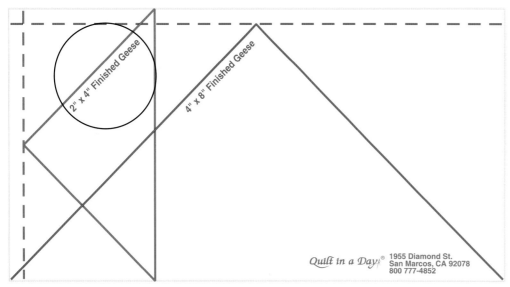

*The Large Geese Ruler can also be used. This ruler is easier to hold onto, but requires one more turning step than the Mini Geese Ruler. When squaring Star Points to 2" x 4" finished size, use **red lines** on Large Geese Ruler. See page 44.*

Squaring Star Points Using Mini Geese Ruler One

1. Cut InvisiGRIP™ ½" smaller than 2½" x 4½" acrylic ruler, and place on under side of ruler.

2. Place patch on small cutting mat.

3. Line up ruler's **green lines** on 45° sewn lines.

Line up ruler's green lines on 45° sewn lines.

4. Line up green dotted line with peak of triangle for ¼" seam allowance.

Line up green dotted line with peak of triangle for ¼" seam allowance.

5. Line up green solid diagonal lines with diagonal seams into corners.

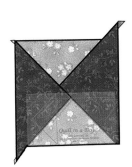

Line up green solid diagonal lines with diagonal seams into corners.

6. Cut block in half to separate into two patches.

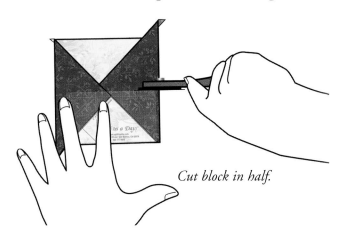

Cut block in half.

7. Hold ruler securely on fabric so it does not shift while cutting. Turning mat, trim off excess fabric on all sides.

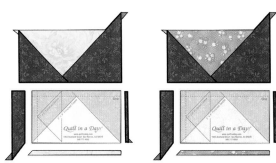

Trim off excess fabric on all sides.

8. Repeat with second half.

Patches should measure 2½" x 4½".

Squaring Star Points Using Large Geese Ruler

1. Cut InvisiGRIP™ ½" smaller than 4½" x 8⅛" acrylic ruler, and place on under side of ruler.

2. Place ruler in vertical position on patch. Line up ruler's **red solid lines** on sewn lines.

3. Line up red dotted line with peak of triangle for ¼" seam allowance. Line up red solid diagonal lines with diagonal seams into corners.

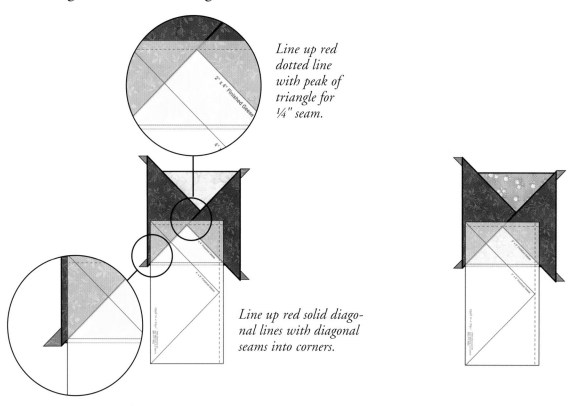

Line up red dotted line with peak of triangle for ¼" seam.

Line up red solid diagonal lines with diagonal seams into corners.

4. Hold ruler securely on fabric so it doesn't shift while cutting.

5. Cut block in half, and separate two patches.

6. Trim off excess fabric on right.

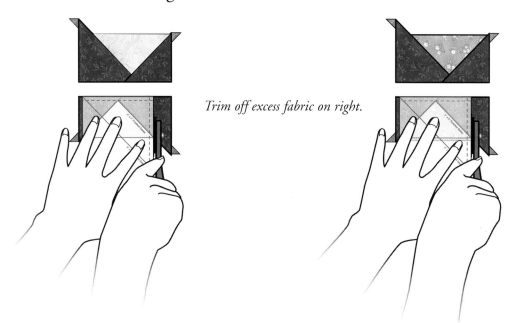

Trim off excess fabric on right.

7. Turn patch.

8. Line up red solid line with bottom of patch.
   Line up green diagonal line on seam.

9. Trim off excess fabric on right and top.

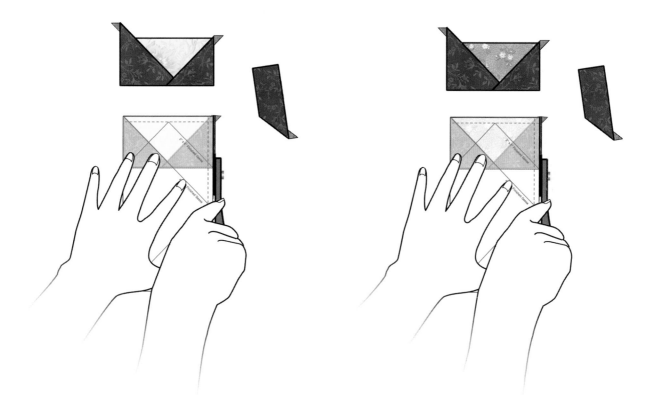

10. Repeat with second half.

 *Patches should measure 2½" x 4½".*

Finishing Stars

1. Stack 4½" Center Squares right side up. You need one for each block.

Number of 4½" Squares	
Wallhanging	4
Crib	6
Lap	12
Twin	15
Square Queen	16
Rectangular Queen	20
California King	25
Dual King	36

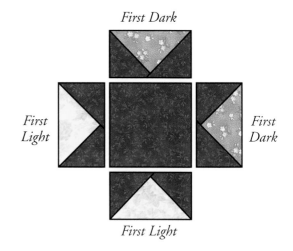

First Dark

First Light

First Dark

First Light

2. Surround Center Squares with First Light Star Points on left and bottom sides and First Dark Star Points on right and top.

3. Place one First Light 2½" Corner Square in bottom left corner and three First Dark 2½" Corner Squares to complete block.

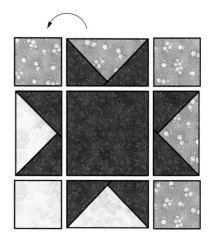

4. Flip top pieces in middle vertical row to vertical row on left, right sides together.

5. Assembly-line sew. Clip every third patch.

If your machine "eats" the corner of your block, use a "jumper scrap" to get it started. Put needle down, pull end threads, and feed with stiletto.

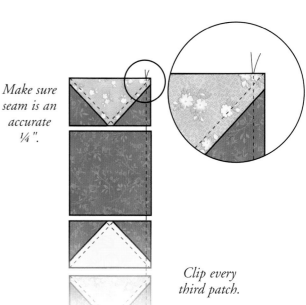

Make sure seam is an accurate ¼".

Clip every third patch.

6. Check for ¼" seam allowance from right side.

7. Open. Flip top pieces on right vertical row onto pieces in middle row.

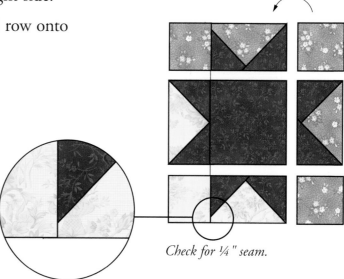

Check for ¼" seam.

8. Assembly-line sew. Open.

9. Clip apart every third patch between blocks.

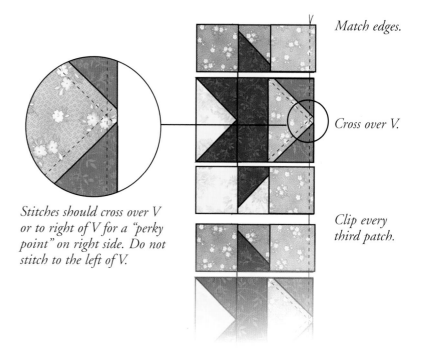

Match edges.

Cross over V.

Clip every third patch.

Stitches should cross over V or to right of V for a "perky point" on right side. Do not stitch to the left of V.

10. Turn.

11. Flip row on right to center row, right sides together.

Check for sharp points on right side.

12. Finger press seams away from Star Points on top and underneath. Lock seams together.

13. Assembly-line sew.

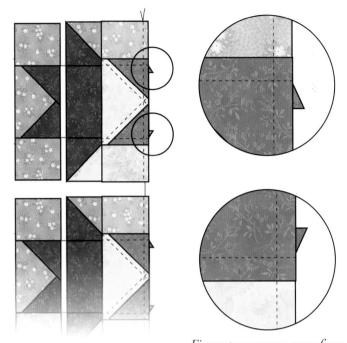

14. Open and turn.

Finger press seams away from Star Points and lock together.

15. Flip remaining row to center row. Finger press seams away from Star Points, locking seams.

16. Assembly-line sew. Hold seams flat with stiletto as you stitch over them.

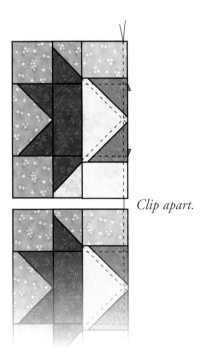

Clip apart.

17. From right side, press just sewn seams away from center.

Check for "perky points" on right side.

18. Check pressing from wrong side.

At this point you should have as many Star Blocks as your finished quilt size calls for.

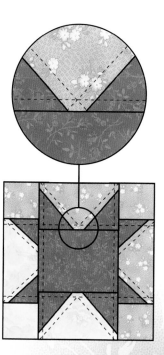

Sewing Strips to Stars

1. Place stacks of 2½" selvage to selvage strips on far left corner of sewing table in alternating order.

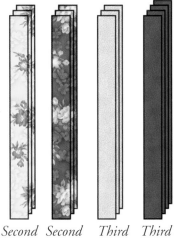

Second   *Second*   *Third*   *Third*
Light   *Dark*   *Light*   *Dark*

Adding Second Light Strip

1. Stack Star blocks right side up with First Dark Corner in upper right.

2. Stack **Second Light strips** right side up to left of sewing machine. Place Star blocks to right of strips.

3. Flip Star right sides together to strip, and line up edges.

4. Sew with ¼" seam. Hold seam allowances flat with stiletto as you sew over them.

5. Place second Star after first Star, and continue to assembly-line sew all Stars.

6. When there is not enough strip left for an additional Star, start a new strip.

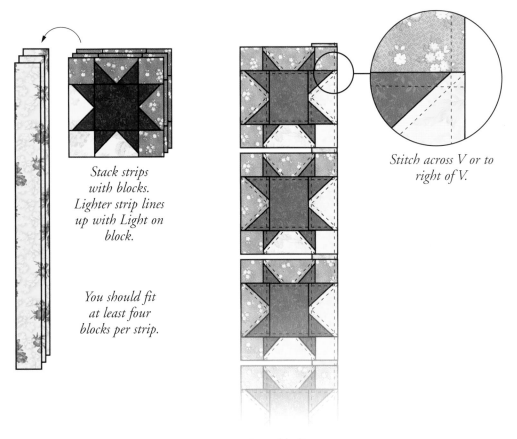

Stack strips with blocks. Lighter strip lines up with Light on block.

You should fit at least four blocks per strip.

Stitch across V or to right of V.

Assembly-line sew.

Cutting Stars Apart

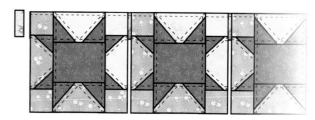

1. Place Stars on cutting mat wrong side up with strip along a grid line.

2. Square off left end, trimming selvages.

Square left end.

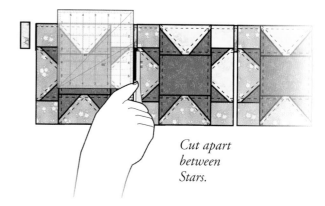

3. Line up 6" Square Up Ruler with ruler's 1" horizontal line on strip, and right edge on edge of block. Cut apart between Stars.

Cut apart between Stars.

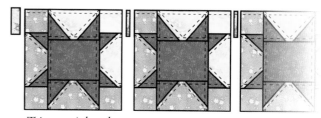

4. Trim if necessary, cutting straight edges.

5. Move to next Star, and continue cutting.

Trim straight edges.

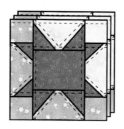

6. Stack wrong side up.

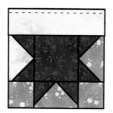

7. Turn stack over.

Setting Seams

Use a pressing mat with marked grid.

1. Place block on pressing mat with Second Light across top, wrong side up. Line up strip with lines on pressing mat.

2. Set seam by pressing **down and up on just sewn strip only**. Do not move iron back and forth.

Place designated fabric on top, and set seam on strip only.

3. Open Second Light strip. Fingerpress strip seam ahead of iron. Use a down and up motion with iron. **Do not press Star**. *Press strip seam only. Pressing whole block with iron after each step of construction distorts blocks.*

Open and press seam toward strip.

4. Check on back side. Seam should be behind Second Light.

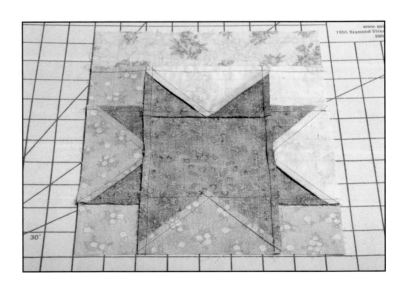

Adding Second Light Again

Each fabric is used twice as strips are sewn counter clockwise around Star.

1. Stack remaining Second Light strips with Star blocks to right.

2. Flip Star right sides together to strip with Second Light on top and perpendicular to new strip.

3. Assembly-line sew.

4. Cut apart between Stars.

5. Stack. Turn stack over.

6. Place block on pressing mat with Second Light across top.

7. Set seam by pressing just sewn seam.

8. Open Second Light strip. Press seam toward Second Light.

9. **Remove extra Second Light from sewing area.**

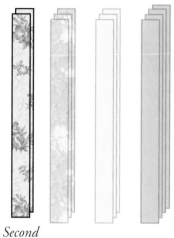

Second Light

The strip just added always goes on top.

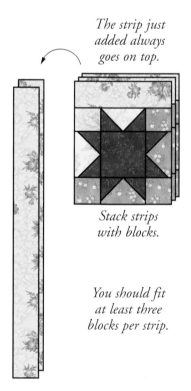

Stack strips with blocks.

You should fit at least three blocks per strip.

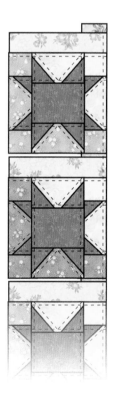

Assembly-line sew and cut apart.

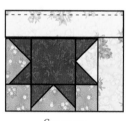

Set seam.

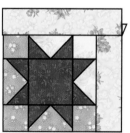

Open and press toward strip.

Adding Second Dark Strip

1. Stack Second Dark strips with Star blocks to right.

2. Flip blocks right sides together to strip with Second Light on top.

3. Assembly-line sew.

4. Cut apart between blocks.

5. Stack. Turn stack over.

6. Place block on pressing mat with Second Dark across top.

7. Set seam. Do not press Star.

8. Open Second Dark strip. Press seam toward Second Dark.

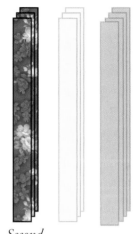

Second Dark

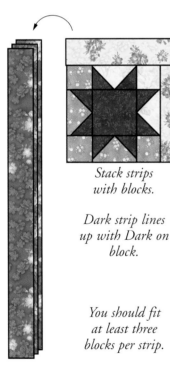

Stack strips with blocks.

Dark strip lines up with Dark on block.

You should fit at least three blocks per strip.

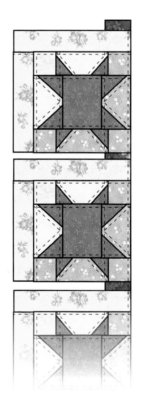

Assembly-line sew and cut apart.

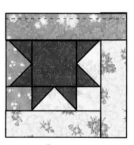

Set seam.

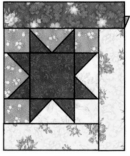

Open and press toward strip.

Adding Second Dark Again

1. Stack remaining Second Dark strips with Star blocks.

2. Flip block right sides together to strip with Second Dark on top.

3. Assembly-line sew.

4. Cut apart between blocks.

5. Stack. Turn stack over.

6. Place block on pressing mat with Second Dark across top.

7. Set seam by pressing just sewn seam only.

8. Open Second Dark strip. Press seam toward Second Dark.

9. **Remove extra Second Dark from sewing area.**

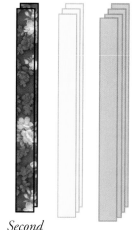

Second Dark

Stack strips with blocks.

You should fit three blocks per strip.

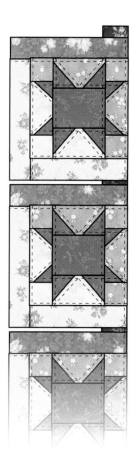

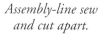

Assembly-line sew and cut apart.

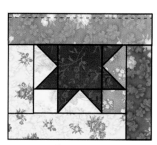

Set seam.

Open and press toward strip.

Adding Third Light Strip

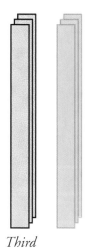

Third Light

1. Stack Third Light strips with blocks.

2. Flip blocks right sides together to strip with Second Dark on top.

3. Assembly-line sew.

4. Cut apart between blocks.

5. Stack. Turn stack over.

6. Place block on pressing mat with Third Light across top.

7. Set seam.

8. Open Third Light strip. Press seam toward Third Light.

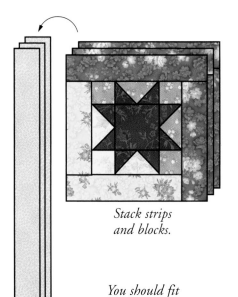

Stack strips and blocks.

You should fit three blocks per strip.

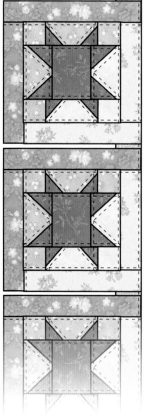

Assembly-line sew and cut apart.

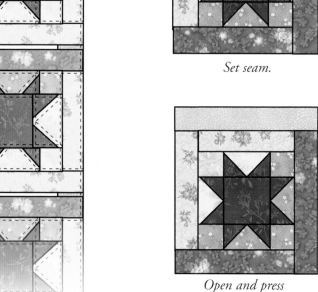

Set seam.

Open and press toward strip.

Adding Third Light Again

1. Stack remaining Third Light strips with blocks.

2. Flip block right sides together to strip with Third Light across top.

3. Assembly-line sew.

4. Cut apart between blocks.

5. Stack. Turn stack over.

6. Place block on pressing mat with Third Light across top.

7. Set seam.

8. Open Third Light strip. Press seam toward Third Light.

9. **Remove extra Third Light from sewing area.**

Third Light

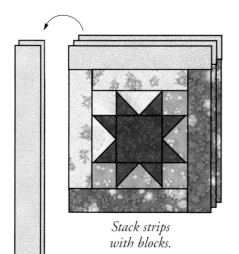

Stack strips with blocks.

You should fit at least two blocks per strip.

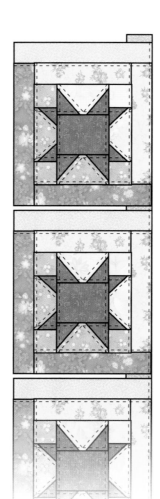

Assembly-line sew and cut apart.

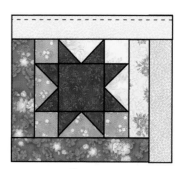

Set seam.

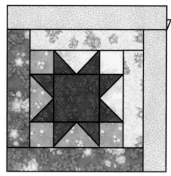

Open and press toward strip.

Adding Third Dark Strip

1.   Stack Third Dark strips with blocks.

2.   Flip blocks right sides together to strip with Third Light across top.

3.   Assembly-line sew.

4.   Cut apart between blocks.

5.   Stack. Turn stack over.

6.   Place block on pressing mat with Third Dark across top.

7.   Set seam.

8.   Open Third Dark strip. Press seam toward Third Dark.

*Third
Dark*

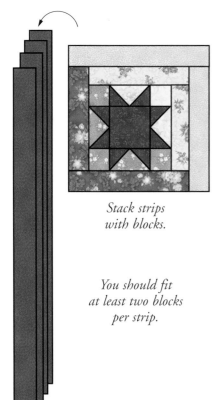

*Stack strips
with blocks.*

*You should fit
at least two blocks
per strip.*

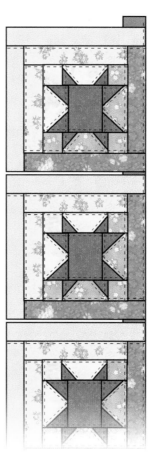

*Assembly-line sew
and cut apart.*

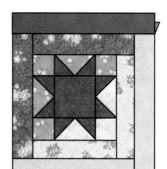

Set seam.

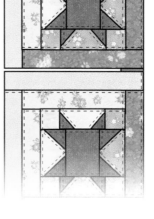

*Open and press
toward strip.*

Adding Third Dark Again

1. Stack remaining Third Dark strips with blocks.

2. Flip block right sides together to strip with Third Dark across top.

3. Assembly-line sew.

4. Cut apart between blocks.

5. Stack. Turn stack over.

6. Place block on pressing mat with Third Dark across top.

7. Set seam.

8. Open Third Dark strip. Press seam toward Third Dark.

9. **Remove extra Third Dark from sewing area.**

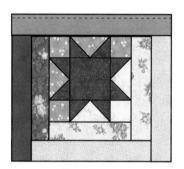

Third Dark

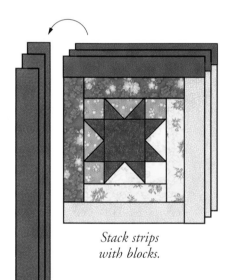

Stack strips with blocks.

You should fit two blocks per strip.

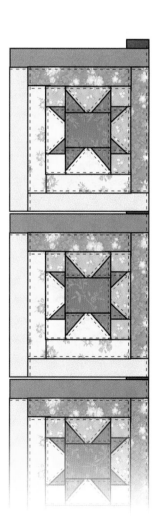

Assembly-line sew and cut apart.

Set seam.

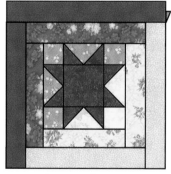

Open and press toward strip.

Choosing Layout

1. Lay out your completed blocks on your bed or on the floor so that you can choose your design. Quilt pattern layouts are on the following pages.

2. Turn blocks into the positions shown for your selected pattern. Use the Third Dark as your guide. If you are having trouble choosing a layout, you may find it helpful to take a digital photo of your blocks in each design you are considering.

Holiday Cheer

Martha selected red and green tone on tone prints to go with snow white stars. Carol quilted large snowflakes in white thread, and then stippled the dark areas with matching thread. Feathers in the outside Border add the final festive touch!

Fields and Furrows

Martha Hernandez
Carol Selepec
45" x 61"

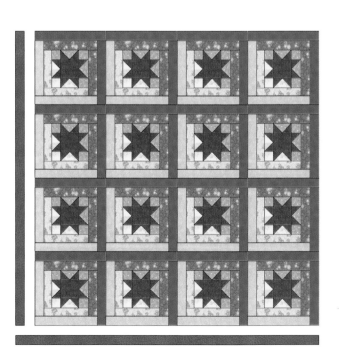

Most blocks, regardless of color combination, look attractive in the Fields and Furrows layout. Think of the Third Dark as Sevens and L's.

*The name of this pattern, All Sevens, refers to the direction of the Third Dark. This pattern looks more complete if you sew extra Third Dark strips on the left and bottom sides **after the quilt top is sewn together**.*

Fields and Furrows

Paisley Delight

Marybeth jazzed up her royal purple stars with a coordinating paisley that sets the blocks spinning. Olive green and beige "logs" calmed the inspirational fabric. A repeat of purple, paisley, and overall quilting completes the charming quilt!

Marybeth Hoag
45" x 61"

All Sevens

The Taj Mahal

Cindi was inspired by the beautiful floral print she used in the Border. It reminded her of a Marrakech Moroccan Spice Market. She chose this setting with the "sunset" on top, dipping into the "dark ocean." To complete the top, she added strips the color of the deep ocean.

Cindi Russell
Shawn York
61" x 77"

Layout Variations

Wallhanging 2 x 2

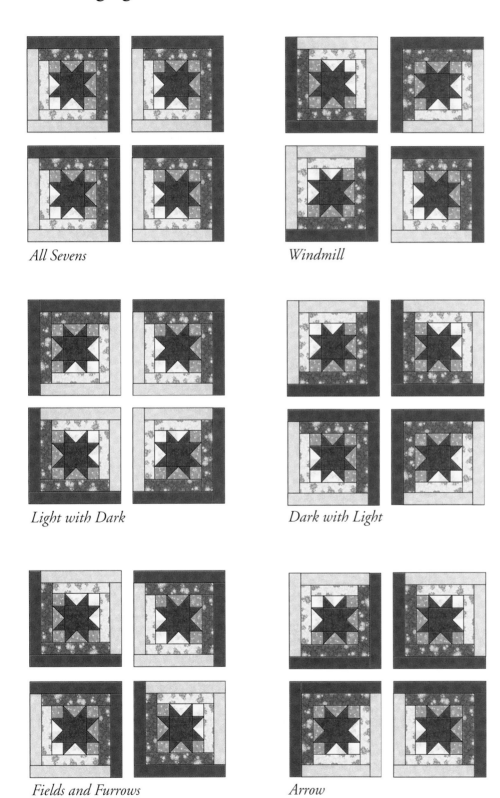

All Sevens

Windmill

Light with Dark

Dark with Light

Fields and Furrows

Arrow

Crib 2 x 3

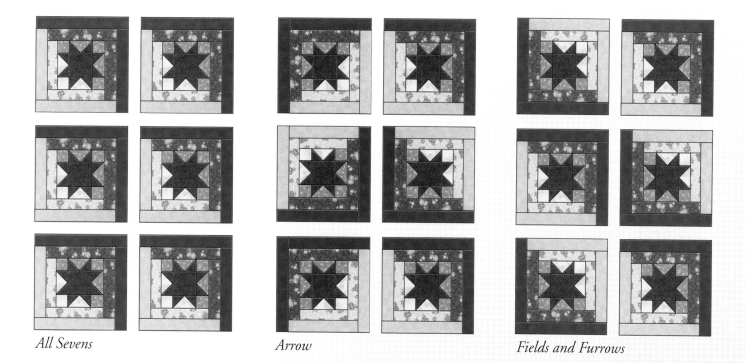

All Sevens

Arrow

Fields and Furrows

Lap 3 x 4

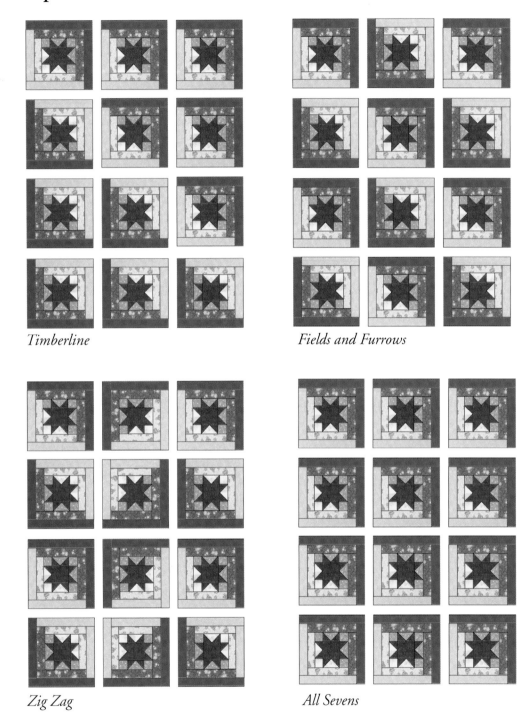

Timberline

Fields and Furrows

Zig Zag

All Sevens

Twin 3 x 5

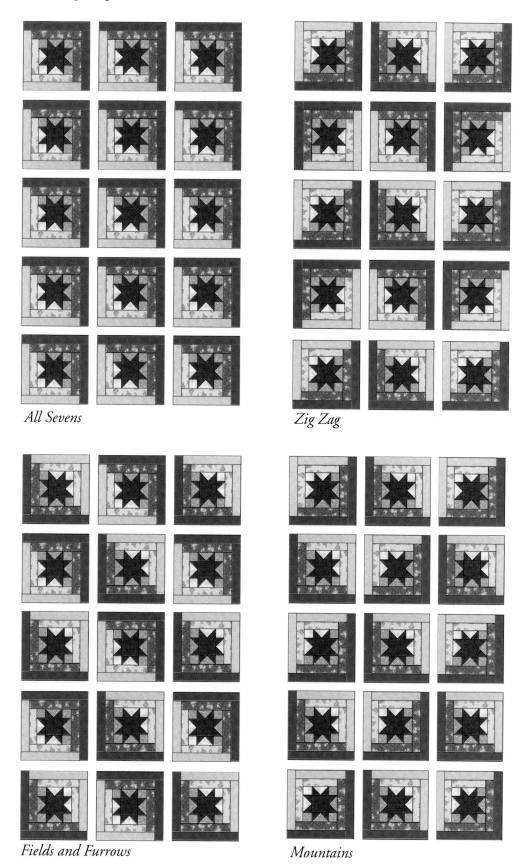

All Sevens

Zig Zag

Fields and Furrows

Mountains

Square Queen 4 x 4 and Dual King 6 x 6

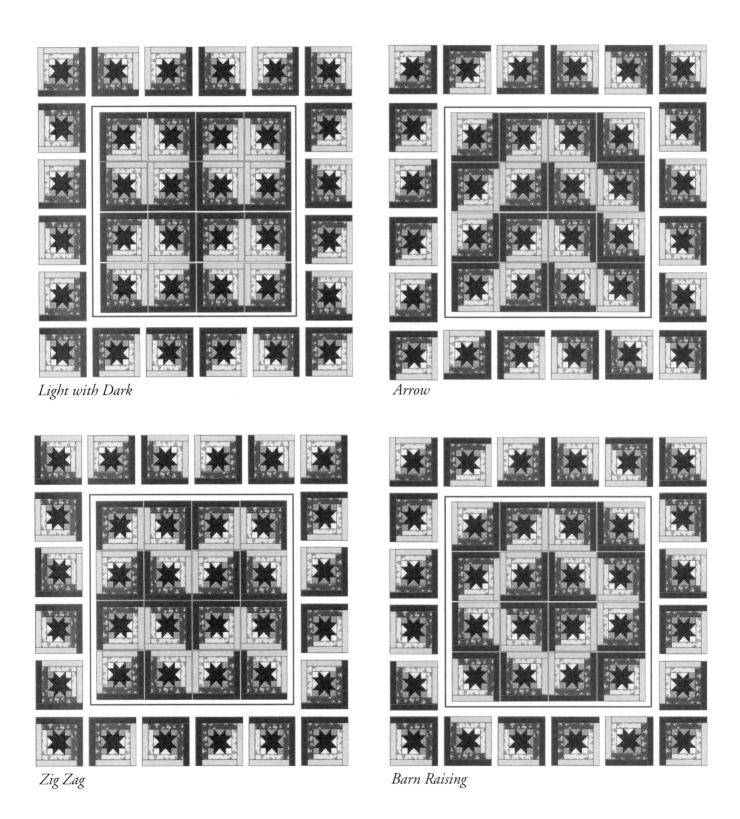

Light with Dark

Arrow

Zig Zag

Barn Raising

Fields and Furrows or All Sevens: See page 68.

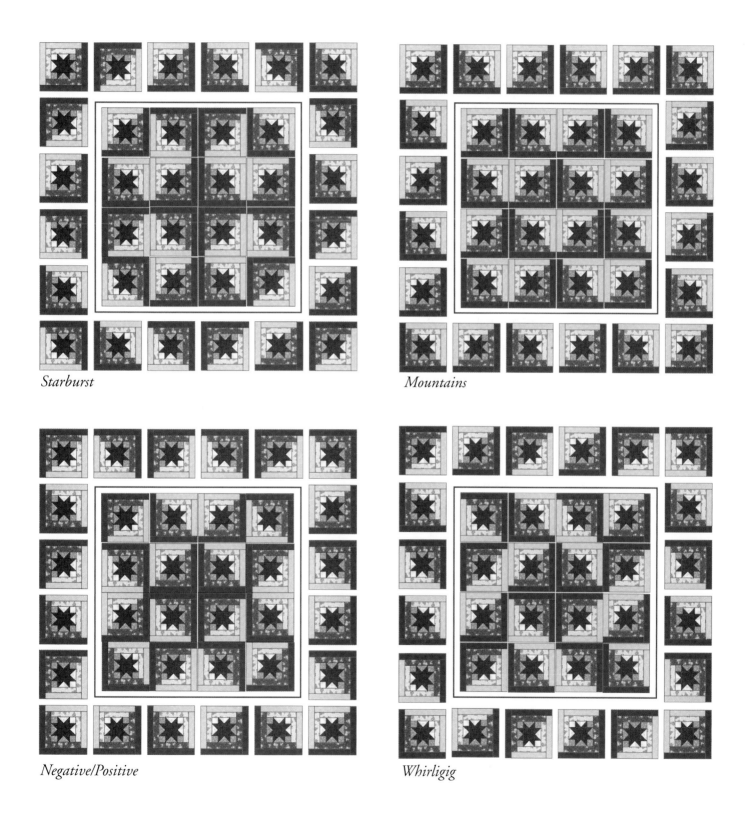

Starburst

Mountains

Negative/Positive

Whirligig

Rectangular Queen 4 x 5 and California King 5 x 5

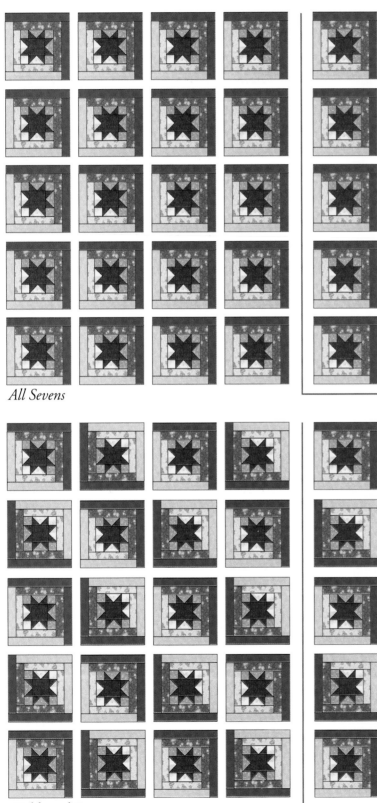

All Sevens

Fields and Furrows

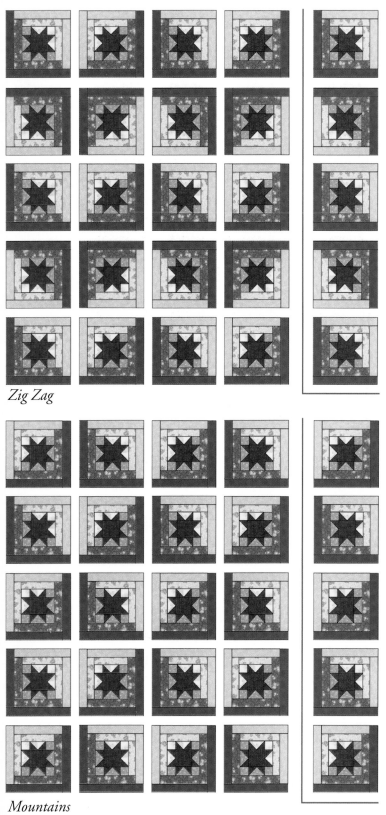

Zig Zag

Mountains

Sewing Top Together

Quilter's Straight Pins

Quilter's straight pins have long shanks and bright green or orange heads for high visibility. Use straight pins to pin blocks together and to pin Borders to your quilt top.

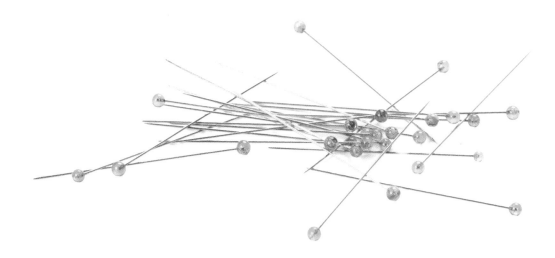

Sewing the First Two Vertical Rows

1. After blocks are laid out in your selected pattern, sew top together in numbered order.

2. Flip second vertical row onto first vertical row right sides together.

3. Starting at the top, pick up blocks from top down, adding each new pair to the bottom of the pile so Blocks 1 and 2 are still on top.

Blocks 1 and 2

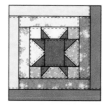

Stack from top down.

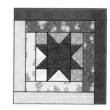

Blocks 3 and 4

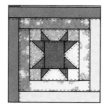

Blocks 5 and 6

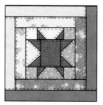

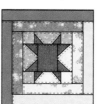

Blocks 7 and 8

4. Take stack of blocks to your sewing machine.

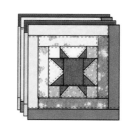

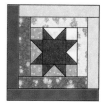

5. Pick up Blocks 1 and 2. Open and check block orientation against layout chart. Flip right sides together.

6. Lock outside edges. Stitch down about 1", maintaining a ¼" seam. This anchors the two together. Finger pin the opposite corners and stretch the two to meet. Stitch. Do not cut threads.

7. Pick up Blocks 3 and 4. Open and check their orientation. Flip them right sides together. Assembly-line sew Blocks 3 and 4 after first two.

8. Continue assembly-line sewing blocks together in first two vertical rows. Backstitch.

   Do not clip the connecting threads.

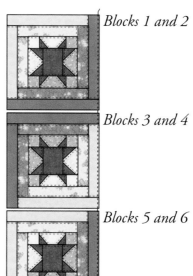

Blocks 1 and 2

Blocks 3 and 4

Blocks 5 and 6

Blocks 7 and 8

Sewing Third Vertical Row

1. Open Rows 1 and 2. Place beside blocks in vertical Row 3.

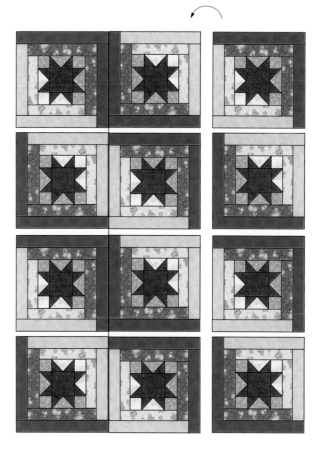

2. Pick up first block in Vertical Row 3, and flip right sides together to Block 2. Pin outside edges of blocks together.

3. Flip next block in Vertical Row 3 right sides together to Block 4. Pin outside edges together.

4. Continue in this manner down third vertical row until all blocks are pinned in place.

5. **Overlap and pin corners of blocks together,** so when you pick up top, blocks are pinned in a chain.

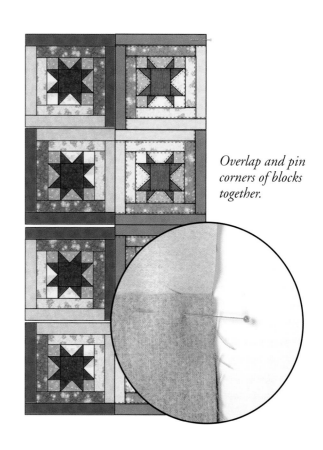

Overlap and pin corners of blocks together.

6. Sew third vertical row to first two vertical rows.

7. Continue pinning and sewing all vertical rows until all blocks are sewn together.

   Do not clip the connecting threads.

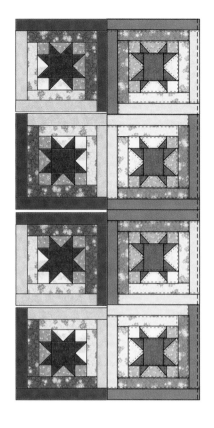

The illustration shows a 12 block quilt as it looks after vertical rows are sewn. Assembly-line sewing, without cutting connecting threads, makes the remaining steps much easier. The connecting threads are equal to pin matching.

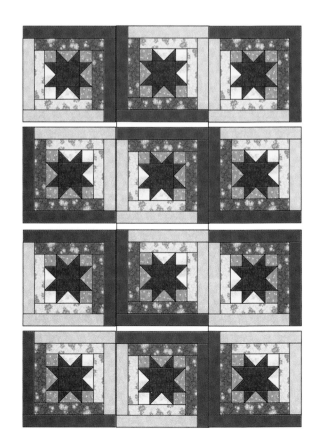

Sewing Horizontal Rows Together

1. Flip top horizontal row down on second horizontal row, with right sides together.

2. Backstitch at beginning and end of row. Stretch and stitch blocks to meet.

3. At connecting thread, push seams in opposite direction. Repeat for every seam in row. When you sew next horizontal row, check direction seams were pressed on the opposite side of the block, and finger press new seams in that direction so seams do not twist.

4. Complete all horizontal rows in same manner, keeping last sewn row on top to check direction of previous seams.

5. Press top from wrong and right side.

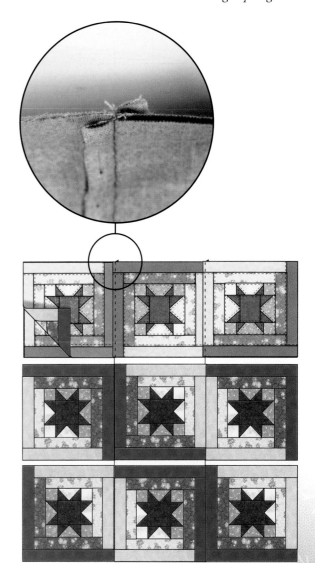

Adding Borders

Piecing Borders

You can custom size your quilt by changing Borders to any width. However, this may affect Backing, Batting, and Binding yardages.

1. Cut Border strips according to your Yardage Chart.

2. Trim selvages.

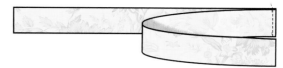

Lay first strip right side up. Lay second strip right sides to it. Backstitch, stitch, and backstitch again.

3. Assembly-line sew into long pieces.

4. Press seams open.

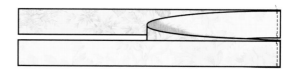

Sewing Borders

1. Measure down center of quilt and sides to find average length. Cut two First Border strips that measurement plus 2".

2. Pin center of strips to center of sides. Extend 1" on each end and pin. Sew with quilt on top.

3. Set seams with First Border on top, open, and press seams toward First Border.

4. Square ends even with top and bottom edges of quilt.

5. Measure width across center and sides, including newly added First Borders. Cut two strips that measurement plus 2".

6. Pin center of strips to top and bottom. Extend 1" on each end and pin. Sew with quilt on top.

7. Press seam toward First Border.

8. Square ends even with side Borders.

9. Repeat with remaining Borders.

Measure, pin, and sew Borders. Press seams toward Border, and square ends.

Adding Folded Border *(Optional)*

It's best if you add a Folded Border after the First Border.

1. If sides of quilt are longer than length of 1¼" Folded Border strips, piece Folded Border strips together.

2. Press 1¼" strips in half lengthwise, **wrong sides together**.

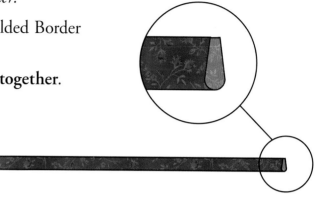

3. Place Folded Border on two opposite sides, matching raw edges.

4. Sew ⅛" seam from raw edge with 10 stitches per inch or 3.0 on computerized machines. Trim even with sides of quilt top. **Do not fold out.**

5. Repeat on remaining two sides, overlapping at corners.

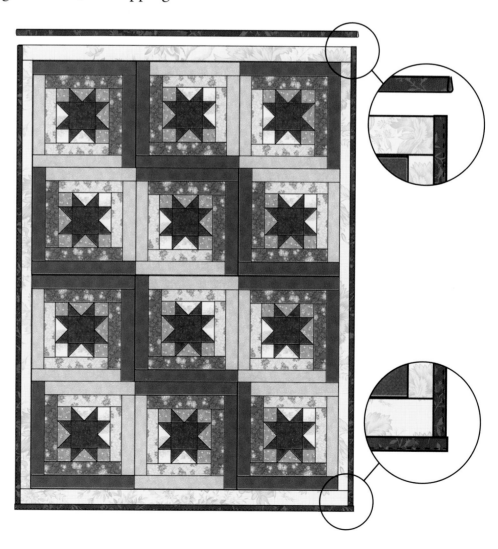

Finishing the Quilt

Customizing Your Backing Using Leftover Fabrics *(Optional)*

Use up leftover fabric by sewing it into your backing. Save fabric by stretching out the width with a center filled with interesting configurations.

1. Identify the straight of grain (stable direction) and cross grain (stretchy direction) of left over fabric by pulling the fabric in both directions. The straight of grain runs parallel to the selvage edge.

2. Always sew stretchy to stretchy and stable to stable.

3. Lay out your quilt top on a bed or on the floor. Place leftover pieces on top to get an idea of how much fabric you need. Place smaller pieces in the center and pieces at least 10" wide along edges.

4. If necessary, purchase more fabric to make up the difference. Place these larger pieces at the top, bottom, and sides.

5. Start working in center of back with smallest pieces. Straighten edges and cut to similar lengths. Sew each piece together, and press. Trim if necessary.

6. Work out from the center, sewing the larger fabrics on the outside edges.

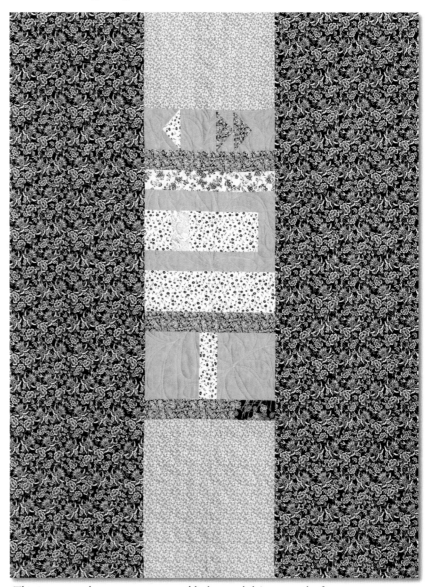

To see the front of this quilt turn to page 11.

This is a great place to put any extra blocks you didn't use on the front.

Long Arm Quilting

Some quilters prefer to complete a top and send it to a long arm quilter. Follow these instructions if long arm quilting is your choice.

1. Clip loose threads. Make sure there are no loose or unsewn seams. Have top free of embellishments.

2. Press top and have it as wrinkle-free as possible. This applies to the backing fabric also.

3. Measure top. Side measurements should be the same, and top and bottom measurements should also be the same.

4. Backing fabric should be 6" longer and wider than quilt top measurements. For example, if the quilt top is 90" x 108", then the backing should be 96" x 114" minimum.

5. The batting should be no less than 6" longer and wider than the pieced top measurements.

6. **Do not pin the three layers together.**

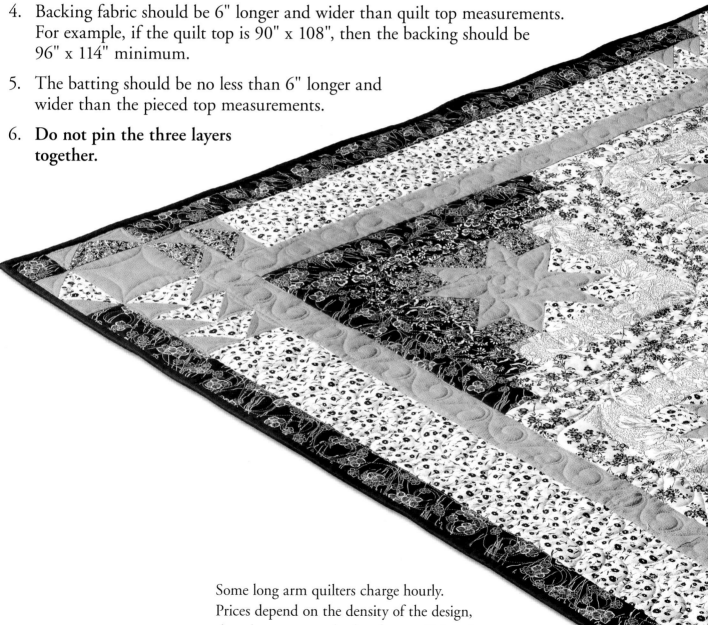

Some long arm quilters charge hourly. Prices depend on the density of the design, thread requests, and other factors. Others base the charge on the square inch size of the quilt. Your local quilt shop can often provide the names of local long arm quilters if you need help locating one.

Quilting on a Conventional Sewing Machine

Layering Your Quilt

1. If necessary, piece Backing approximately 4" to 6" larger than finished top.

2. Spread out Backing on a large table or floor area, **right side down**. Clamp fabric to edge of table with quilt clips, or tape Backing to the floor. Do not stretch Backing.

3. Layer Batting on Backing, also 4" to 6" larger than finished top. Pat flat.

4. With right side up, center quilt on Batting and Backing. Smooth until all layers are flat. Clamp or tape outside edges.

Safety Pinning

1. Place pin covers on 1" safety pins with pliers.

2. Pin away from where you plan to quilt. Catch tip of pin in grooves on pinning tool, and close pins.

3. Safety pin through all layers three to five inches apart.

4. Use pinning tool to open pins when removing them. Store pins opened.

"Stitch in the Ditch" along Blocks and Borders

1. Thread your machine with matching thread or invisible thread. If you use invisible thread, loosen your top tension. Match the bobbin thread to the Backing.

2. Attach your walking foot, and lengthen the stitch to 8 to 10 stitches per inch or 3.0 or 3.5 on computerized machine.

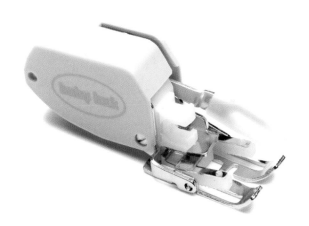

3. Roll corner of quilt to first Star. Hold "roll" in place with quilt clamps. Place hands on quilt in triangular shape, and spread seams open. Stitch in the ditch, anchoring Stars.

4. For large sizes, "free motion" stitch around Stars so you don't have to continuously turn quilt.

Stitch in the ditch around Star.

5. Stitch ¼" away from "logs".

6. Stitch in the ditch along Border seams.

Stitch ¼" from "logs".

Marking for Free Motion Quilting

1. Select an appropriate continuous line stencil.

2. Center on area to be quilted, and trace lines with disappearing marker. An alternative method is lightly spraying fabric with water, and pouncing powder into lines of stencil.

The Stencil Company
HOL-461-04

Quilting with Darning Foot

1. Attach darning foot to sewing machine. Drop feed dogs or cover feed dogs with a plate. No stitch length is required as you control the length by your sewing speed. Use a fine needle and regular thread in the top and regular thread to match the Backing in the bobbin. Use needle down position.

2. Place hands flat around marked design. Bring bobbin thread up on line.

3. Lock stitch and clip thread tails. Free motion stitch **on marked lines**. Keep top of block at top. Sew sideways and back and forth without turning quilt.

4. Lock stitches and cut threads.

Center continuous line stencil on Star, and trace inside lines.

Stitch on lines with darning foot and matching thread.

Adding Binding

1. Square off selvage edges on 3" Binding strips. Assembly-line sew short ends to make one continuous strip.

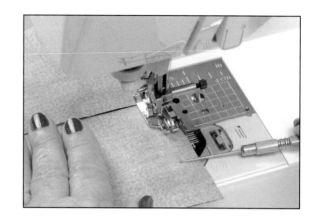

2. Press seams open.

3. Fold and press in half lengthwise with **wrong sides together**.

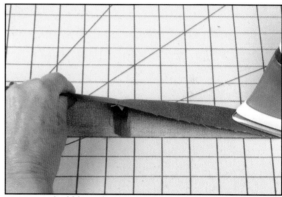

Press in half lengthwise with wrong sides together.

4. Place walking foot attachment on sewing machine, and regular thread on top and in bobbin to match Binding.

5. In middle of one side, line up raw edges of folded Binding with raw edges of quilt. Begin stitching 4" from end of Binding. Sew with 10 stitches per inch, or 3.0 to 3.5. Sew approximately ⅜" from edge, or width of walking foot.

Sew with 10 stitches per inch.

6. Place pin ⅜" from corner of quilt.

7. At corner, stop stitching at pin ⅜" in from edge with needle in fabric. Raise presser foot and turn quilt toward corner.

8. Put presser foot down. Stitch diagonally off edge of Binding.

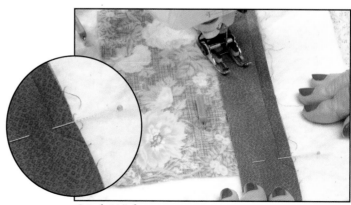

Stitch ⅜" from corner.

9. Raise foot, and pull quilt forward slightly.

10. Turn quilt to next side. Remove pin.

11. Fold Binding strip straight up on diagonal. Fingerpress diagonal fold.

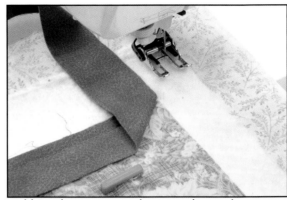

Fold Binding strip straight up on diagonal.

12. Fold Binding strip straight down with diagonal fold underneath. Line up top of fold with raw edge of Binding underneath.

Fold Binding strip straight down.

13. Begin sewing from edge.

14. Continue stitching and mitering corners around outside of quilt.

15. Stop stitching 4" from where ends will overlap.

16. Line up two ends of Binding. Trim excess with ½" overlap.

17. Pull ends away from quilt. Line up newly cut edges.

18. Sew a ¼" seam.

19. Press seam open.

20. Continue stitching Binding in place.

21. Trim Batting and Backing up to ⅛" from raw edges of Binding.

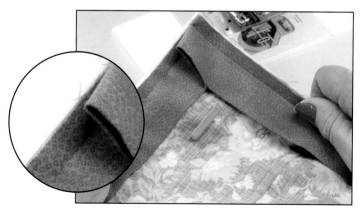

22. Fold back Binding.

23. Pull Binding to back side of quilt.

24. Pin in place so that folded edge on Binding covers stitching line. Tuck in excess fabric at each miter on diagonal.

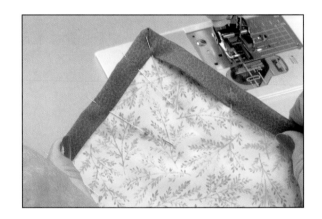

25. From right side, "stitch in the ditch" using invisible or matching thread on front side, and bobbin thread to match Binding on back side. Catch folded edge of Binding on the back side with stitching.

   Optional: Hand stitch Binding in place.

26. Hand stitch miters.

27. Sew identification label on Back.

   • name of maker
   • place where quilt was made
   • year
   • name of quilt
   • any other pertinent information.

Pillow Shams

Making Shams

1. Hem one 28" side on backing pieces.

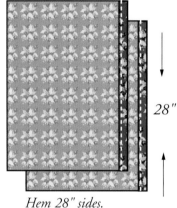

Hem 28" sides.

2. Place backing pieces right sides together to top piece, overlapping hems in center. Match outside edges. Pin.

3. Place on top of batting, with backing wrong side up. Pin.

4. Sew ¼" seam around outside edge.

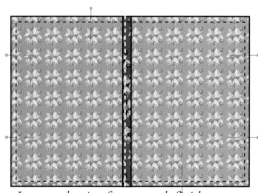

Layer on batting for a smooth finish.

Finishing Sham

1. Turn right side out.

2. Mark stitching line 3" from outside edge.

3. Quilt on line with 3.0 or 3.5 stitch length.

4. Stuff with pillow.

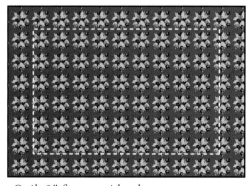

Quilt 3" from outside edge.

Scrappy Lap Quilt with Pillow Case

61" x 77"
Twelve 16" Blocks
3 x 4

*Use one Jelly Roll and One Layer Cake
or the equivalent in scraps, plus yardage
for Stars and First Border.*

*Martha Hernandez
Amie Potter
61" x 77"*

*Ten inch squares from Layer Cake are for scrappy single triangles in Star Points and Star Corners. The
remaining 10" squares become a scrappy Border, Binding and Pillow Case. Sort 10" Layer Cake Squares
as directed. The Jelly Roll is for scrappy "logs" of Second and Third Lights and Darks.*

Stars	1 yd
Star Points	(3) 7" strips cut into (12) 7" squares
Star Centers	(2) 4½" strips cut into (12) 4½" squares
First Light	
Star Points	(6) different 10" squares
First Dark	
Star Points	(6) different 10" squares
Scrappy Second Border	(14) different 10" squares

First Border	½ yd
	(6) 2½" strips
Binding	(10) different 10" squares
Backing	4½ yds
Batting	69" x 85"

Pillow Case

Body of Pillow Case	(6) different 10" squares
Cuff	⅓ yd (1) 10" strip
Backing	¾ yd

Cutting Star Points and Corner Squares

1. Cut up six different 10" squares First Light. Stack same fabrics together.

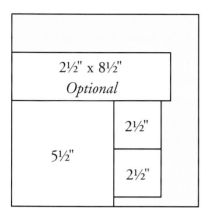

Light Single Triangles for Star Points
(1) 5½" square

Star Corners
(2) 2½" squares

Second Light Strip
(1) 2½" x 8½"
(Optional - Set aside for blocks.)

2. Cut six different 10" squares First Dark. Stack same fabrics together.

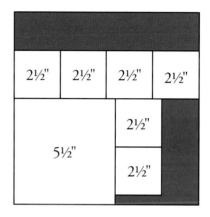

Dark Single Triangles for Star Points
(1) 5½" square

Star Corners
(6) 2½" squares

Making Stars

1. Divide 7" squares for Star Points into two stacks of six each.

2. Stack six different 5½" squares First Light with left stack.

3. Stack six different 5½" squares First Dark with right stack.

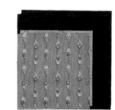

5½" First Light with 7" Star Points

5½" First Dark with 7" Star Points

4. Sew Star Points following directions on pages 34 – 45.

5. Lay out a total of twelve Stars. For variety, place pairs of First Light Star Points with pairs of different First Dark Star Points.

  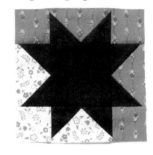 

6. Sew Stars together following directions beginning on page 46.

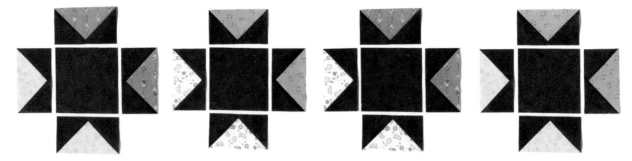

Adding Strips

1. Sort 2½" Jelly Roll strips (or scraps) by color.

2. Lay out Stars. Place strips beside blocks to continue Light and Dark sides.

3. Cut pieces to size for each block, and place beside Star block.

Second Light Strips	(1) 2½" x 8½"
	(1) 2½" x 10½" *Same or different*
Third Light Strips	(1) 2½" x 12½"
	(1) 2½" x 14½" *Same or different*
Second Dark Strips	(1) 2½" x 10½"
	(1) 2½"x 12½" *Same or different*
Third Dark Strips	(1) 2½" x 14½"
	(1) 2½" x 16½" *Same or different*

4. Sew strips to blocks following illustrations beginning on page 50.

5. Sew blocks together three across and four down.

6. Sew 2½" First Border to top, following directions on page 76.

Making Scrappy Second Border

1. Count out fourteen different 10" squares in a mix of colors.

2. Pull each square to determine which way is stretchy, and which way is stable. Place stretch up and down.

3. Cut in half into 5" x 10" pieces, and make two identical stacks.

4. Take one stack and sew together narrow end to narrow end. Press seams to one side.

5. Make identical strip with second stack. Press seams in one direction.

6. Pin and sew one Border to right side, beginning at top.

7. Trim excess and set aside. Sew to bottom after left side Border is added.

8. Pin and sew identical Border to left side, beginning at bottom.

9. Trim excess. Continuing with same strip, sew to top.

10. Layer and quilt, beginning on page 80.

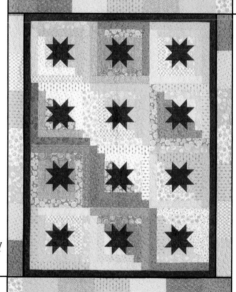

Stretch

Start here with first strip set.

Start here with second strip set.

Making Binding

1. Lay out ten different 10" squares.

2. Determine which way is stretchy, and place stretch up and down.

3. Cut each square into three 3" x 10" rectangles.

4. Piece narrow ends together into one strip, mixing up fabrics. Press seams open.

5. Press in half wrong sides together the length of the strip.

6. Sew Binding to quilted top, beginning on page 83.

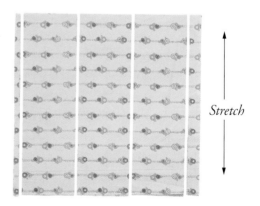

Stretch

Making Pillow Case

Sewing Front

1. Piece center strip together from left-overs into 2½" x 30" strip.

2. Piece six different 10" squares into two rows of three each.

3. Place center strip with 10" squares.

4. Piece together, and press seams to center strip.

5. Trim approximately 3½" from Cuff end so length of Pillow Case is 25".

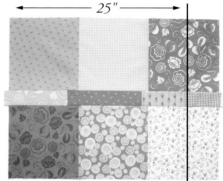

Trim approximately 3½" from Cuff end.

Lining Pillow Case

1. Cut Backing fabric into two pieces same as Pillow Case front, about 20½" x 25".

2. Stack two Backing pieces right side up.

3. Place Pillow front right sides together to layered Backings.

4. Pin around sides and bottom.

5. Backstitch, sew around sides and bottom, and backstitch.

6. Insert hand inside Pillow Case, grasp front, and turn right side out.

7. Pull out corners with stiletto. Press edges flat.

8. Pull Backings apart. Pin one Back onto Pillow Case front at Cuff end. This Backing lines the patchwork so seams do not fray with washing and wear.

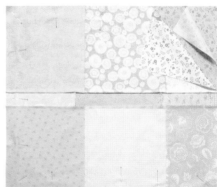

Two Backings right side up

Cuff end

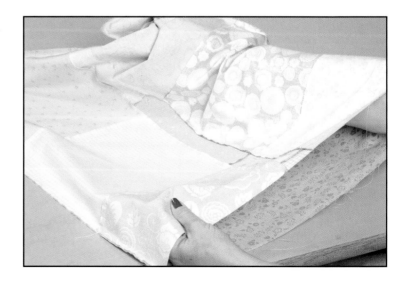

Finishing Pillow Case

1. Piece leftover 2½" strips together into a 2½" x 45" strip for Folded Border.

2. Press in half wrong sides together.

3. Trim to same width as Pillow Case, including seams.

4. Match raw edges of Folded Border and 10" Cuff. Sew with seam slightly less than ¼".

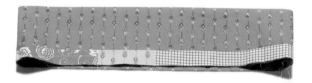

5. Press in half lengthwise, wrong sides together.

6. Open. Matching Folded Border, sew short ends right sides together into a "tube." Press seam open.

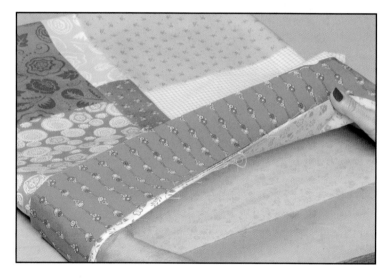

7. Refold "tube" right side out. Folded Border is on inside of "tube."

8. Slip "tube" over end of Pillow Case. Match side seams and raw edges. Pin around circle.

9. Sew with ¼" seam.

10. Zigzag stitch for a clean finished edge.

11. Open Cuff.

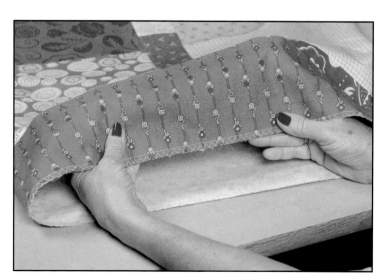

Index

Order Information

Quilt in a Day books offer a wide range of techniques and are directed toward a variety of skill levels. If you do not have a quilt shop in your area, you may write or call for a complete catalog and current price list of all books and patterns published by Quilt in a Day®, Inc.

Quilt in a Day
1955 Diamond St.
San Marcos, CA 92078
800 777-4852
www.quiltinaday.com

Best Sellers

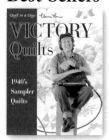

Victory Quilts
Item # 1078

Lover's Knot
Item # 1079

Day & Night
Quilts
Item # 1080

Log Cabin
Item # 1042

Egg Money Quilts
Item # 1073

Quick Trip Quilts
Item # 1076

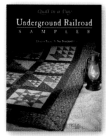

Underground
Railroad
Item # 1068

Quilts Through
the Seasons
Item # 1075

Still Stripping
Item # 1069

Sunbonnet Sue
Item # 1023

Irish Chain
Item # 1072

Magic Vine Quilt
Item # 1077

Acknowledgements

Thanks to our stars!

Quilt Piecers

Sue Bouchard
Jimna Burns
Angela Castro
Anne Dease
Ann Drothler
Marie Harper
Karyn Helsel
Martha Hernandez
Marybeth Hoag
Judy Knoechel

Linda Parker
Karen Pavone
Cindi Russell
LuAnn Stout
Teresa Varnes

Long Arm Quilters

Robin Kinley
Amie Potter
Carol Selepec
Phyllis Strickland
Shawn York

Angela Castro
Carol Selepec
96" x 96"